Bit, Bat, Bee, Rime with Me!

Word Patterns and Activities, Grades K-3

Linda Armstrong

Linworth Publishing, Inc.
Columbus, Ohio

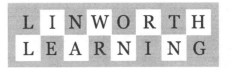

Library of Congress Cataloging-in-Publication Data

Armstrong, Linda.
Bit, bat, bee, rime with me! word patterns and activities, grades K-3 / Linda Armstrong.
p. cm.
Includes bibliographical references and index.
ISBN-13: 978-1-58683-336-7 (pbk.)
ISBN-10: 1-58683-336-7 (pbk.)
1. English language—Rhyme—Study and teaching (Early childhood)—Activity programs. 2. Rhyming games. 3. Language arts (Early childhood) I. Title.
LB1139.5.L35A76 2009
372.6—dc22

                                                            2008041349

Cynthia Anderson: Editor
Judi Repman: Consulting Editor

Published by Linworth Publishing, Inc.
3650 Olentangy River Road
Suite 250
Columbus, Ohio 43214

ISBN 13: 978-1-58683-336-7
ISBN 10: 1-58683-336-7

5 4 3 2 1

Table of Contents

Table of Contents (continued)

Table of Contents (continued)

Table of Contents (continued)

Table of Contents (continued)

Table of Contents (continued)

Table of Contents (continued)

Table of Contents

Table of Contents (continued)

Table of Contents (continued)

Table of Contents (continued)

Table of Figures

Table of Figures (continued)

About the Author

Before moving to Colorado, Linda Armstrong was an educator in Los Angeles. She served first as a classroom teacher, and later as a Language Development Resource Teacher based in the school library. She told stories in costume, presented puppet shows, sponsored a drama club, and coordinated a school-wide Language Arts festival.

Now, Linda writes books for children and their teachers. Her credits include more than 20 adaptations of classic stories, a collection of contemporary free verse, a middle grade novel, a book of art projects for elementary teachers, and several phonics books. She has also written supplementary classroom materials for language arts, history, reading comprehension, and math.

Previous books in this series include *1, 2, 3 Follow Me: Math Puzzles and Rhymes, Grades K-1*, and *ABC, Follow Me! Phonics, Rhymes, and Crafts, Grades K-1*.

Acknowledgments

I wish to thank my walking partner and fellow Linworth author Jane Heitman for her suggestions and encouragement. I would also like to thank my husband, Alden, for his patience.

Dedication

For my mother, who started me on the road to reading.

Introduction

WHAT IS A RIME?

Rimes are word families that share final sounds and spellings. For example, rime and time are rimes. Rhyme and thyme are also rhymes, but rime and thyme are not.

WHY ARE RIMES IMPORTANT?

Rimes, because of their consistency, help students see how letters, and their corresponding phonemes, work to differentiate one written word from another. For example, by examining the difference between dog and hog, children discover how the sounds of /d/ and /h/ change an animal that barks into one that grunts.

WHO NEEDS THIS BOOK?

■ *Teachers*

After mastering letter forms (graphemes) and letter sounds (phonemes), many students are ready to utilize rimes to decode families of familiar words. For this reason, reading standards in many states require children to recognize them. This book capitalizes on children's natural enjoyment of verse to enhance phoneme and word recognition skills.

■ *Librarians*

Like other Linworth Learning books, *Bit, Bat, Bee, Rime with Me! Word Patterns and Activities, Grades K-3* is designed to mesh library resources with classroom curricula. A helpful list of rhyming picture books and easy readers relates word pattern skills to favorite stories. Also included in this volume is a list of professional resources related to rime, and a list of materials related to indoor and outdoor games.

Rhymes and short plays in this book can be used to enhance library story hour programs. Related rhyming and non-rhyming picture books are suggested to accompany many of the activities. A variety of handy indexes enable busy librarians to assist patrons quickly and easily.

■ *Parents and Grandparents*

After helping children learn their letters and sounds, parents are often eager to offer additional coaching. Many of the verses and activities in this book are perfect for car rides and rainy days. They are fun as well as educational. Bibliographies provide an introduction to additional materials in library collections and on the Internet.

HOW THIS BOOK IS ARRANGED

There are many rimes in English. The rime families in this book include words commonly found in texts and vocabulary lists from grades K-3. The first section of *Bit, Bat, Bee* features short vowel words (cvc or cvcc). The second half of the book contains long vowel words (cvce or cvvc).

Each verse is prefaced by a brief introduction. Many verse pages include suggested movements and interactive performance suggestions. All activity pages include required materials, procedures, and optional extensions.

SPECIAL FEATURES OF THIS BOOK

- More than 30 original verses

- Easy color, cut, and fold projects with patterns. Target words are printed on each pattern so participants can share what they have learned with friends and relatives after the session.

- Simple teaching games and activities for the classroom and a bibliography of teaching game resources

- A table of common rime families for sliders, word cards, or games

- Simple patterns for rime sliders

- Two-character mini-plays and easy, low-mess puppet patterns

- A list of useful Web sites

- A bibliography of rhyming picture books to help children hear end sounds

- A bibliography of related resources for teachers, librarians, and other professionals

PAINLESS WAYS TO BUILD RIME AWARENESS

■ *Verse*

Bit, Bat, Bee, Rime with Me! Word Patterns and Activities, Grades K-3 provides lively, original verses which target groups of pattern words. Most include accompanying actions such as pantomime, clapping, nodding, or swaying. A specific craft or game, with instructions, follows each poem.

■ Outdoor Challenges

Red Rover and other traditional playground games feature rimes. Encourage children to hear and say the rhyming words as part of the game, and then invite them to take the task a step further by reading the lyrics. Use the provided rime lists to invent simple new games.

Directions for Call Ball and other variations on old favorites are indexed in this book's Table of Rhymes, Games, and Activities. Ideas for traditional playground games can be found in the library or online. For example, the rules for Red Rover are available at <www.gameskidsplay.net/games/strength_games/redrover.htm>.

■ Writing

Since rimes apply to spelling as well as reading, students will soon acquire a store of words to use in their stories. Invite students to start including these words in written work with simple cloze activities. For example, use copies of the rhymes in this book. Simply cover the second rime in each verse and add a blank line for the student response before reproducing the page.

Second and third graders might enjoy completing special two-word rhymes called "hink pinks." Provide a riddle clue and the first word in a rime pair. Here is an example. What do you call a hound that loves swamps? A bog _____ (dog).

After children are familiar with the words, abandon the emphasis on their rhyming aspects and use them as inspiration for short pieces of writing. For example, after learning words in the –*ill* rime family, students might look at a picture of a hill and write a short paragraph about what is on the other side.

■ Personal Spelling Dictionaries

If children keep personal spelling dictionaries to use when they compose stories, encourage them to add featured rime family words to their lists.

■ Songs

Once students have acquired a number of words, challenge them to write silly verses of their own. These are not, of course, to be confused with real poetry, but they are great fun and children enjoy sharing them.

One way to do this is to start with a favorite song and change the words. As an example, share the original version of "On Top of Old Smoky" along with that timeless summer camp classic "On Top of Spaghetti."

The trick here is to keep it very short. Do not try to do the whole song. One verse is plenty. Children can do this activity individually, in small groups, or as a short teacher-led classroom project.

■ Word Hunts

Encourage students to find individual words from the day's featured rime family in classroom texts as well as in library books. The advantage of a text is that each reader has a copy of the same book. It just takes a minute to challenge students to find a word such as "can" on a page. Children can help each other to locate the target word.

As a variation, children can count how many times a common word such as "will" or "not" appears on a page. If you do not have textbooks, use copies of a school bulletin or the school newspaper. If you choose a high-frequency word, it will not matter that the material is written at a much higher grade level.

■ Indoor Games

Many card games such as War, Snap, and Rummy involve matching. Use a computer, printer, and the word lists to create a set of 52 rime cards with four cards in each rhyming set. Avoid unfamiliar or nonsense words. Encourage children to read the words in the pair or set aloud before completing each play. Standard game rules are available at <www.usplayingcard.com/gamerules/childrenscardgames.html>.

Use the simple board games in your closet to reinforce rime recognition. Instruct players to read a word from a slider or a word card before throwing their dice.

■ *Picture Books, Stories, and Poems*

Reading aloud to children is a wonderful practice whether at home, in the classroom, or in the library. Many beloved picture books and early readers feature rimes. Encourage story hour groups to participate during readings by allowing them to supply rhyming pattern words in such predictable tales as *The Cat in the Hat* and *Hop on Pop*.

Children should listen to stories and verses for enjoyment. To appreciate the full power of rimes, however, they must see the word families in print and use them, along with context and other cues to read.

Without turning your story session into a drill or chore, review a few target rimes on a whiteboard, a flannel board, or other visual device after the reading. Later, invite children to share books that feature rimes with peers, adult volunteers, or older children. A special rack or table display can help.

The idea is to enable young readers to spot words they have met as rimes within text. With experience, they should be able to utilize rime families, along with phonemes and other clues, to read with increasing confidence and independence.

■ *Spotting Rime Family Words in Text*

There are other ways to encourage students to become more conscious of rime family words appearing in text. Here are a few:

- Change stories into plays for students to present as Reader's Theater. Include recently featured rime family words.

- Provide riddles and jokes with several characters that require students to read aloud.

- Arrange poetry readings. Groups of three or four students can work together to read a short poem. Each participant reads a line. Readers help each other with decoding, a brief rehearsal, and presentation. For extra impact, videotape the event and play the DVD at a parent event.

Table of Arts and Crafts Projects

Table of Rhymes, Games, and Activities

Table of Rhymes, Games, and Activities (continued)

Bibliography of Game and Activity Books for Children

Blevins, Wiley. *Phonemic Awareness Activities for Early Reading Success (Grades K-2)*. New York: Scholastic, 1999. Carefully designed games enrich the clear lesson plans in this useful book, which also includes bibliographies and other resources.

Burch, Marilyn Myers. *Instant File-Folder Games for Reading*. New York: Instructor Books, 2001. File-folder games are great for independent use at learning centers. Check out this resource for inspiration, and then make your own rime folder activities.

Feldman, Jean R. *Complete Handbook of Indoor and Outdoor Games and Activities for Young Children*. San Francisco: Jossey-Bass, 1994. With 370 quick, age-appropriate game ideas, how can you miss?

Forrest, Sandy, and Debra Wise. *Readers Digest Great Big Book of Children's Games—Over 450 Indoor and Outdoor Games for Kids*. Pleasantville: Readers Digest, 1999. This terrific volume will help you create a game to suit any teaching need.

Foster, David R., James L. Overholt, and Ron Schultz. *Indoor Action Games for Elementary Children: Active Games and Academic Activities for Fun and Fitness*. New York: Parker Publishing Company, 1989. Associate movement with other cues, and create powerful teaching tools. Find great ideas here.

Goodman, Lori, and Lora Myers. *Wordplay: Fun Games for Building Reading and Writing Skills in Children with Learning Difficulties*. New York: McGraw-Hill, 2004. Find a treasure trove of multisensory teaching ideas in this book.

Hale, James, and Michelle Ramsey. *Phonics Games Kids Can't Resist! (Grades K-2)*. New York: Scholastic Teaching Resources, 2000. Find a wealth of great hands-on activities for beginning readers here.

Julio, Susan. *15 Fun and Easy Games for Young Learners Reading: Reproducible, Easy-to-Play Learning Games That Help Kids Build Essential Reading Skills*. Chicago: Scholastic Professional Books, 2001. Use this book to create practical learning center materials for follow-up and review.

Kaye, Peggy. *Games for Reading*. New York: Pantheon, 1984. This classic book contains 70 great games to help children master important reading skills without drudgery.

LeFevre, Dale N. *Best New Games: 77 Games and 7 Trust Activities for All Ages and Abilities*. Champaign, IL: Human Kinetics Publishers, 2001. These non-competitive games are sure to inspire you.

Linse, Caroline. *20 Fun-Filled Games That Build Early Reading Skills (Grades K-2)*. New York: Scholastic, 2001. This resource includes ready-to-use game boards.

Luvmour, Josette, and Sambhava Luvmour. *Win-Win Games for All Ages: Cooperative Activities for Building Social Skills*. Gabriola Island, BC: New Society Publishers, 2002. Check out this book for creative classroom ideas.

Novelli, Joan. *30 Wonderful Word Family Games: With Pull-Out Poster Game*. Chicago: Scholastic Professional Books, 2002. This book contains practical, enjoyable reading games for individual, partner, and group use.

Sugar, Kim Kostoroski, and Steve Sugar. *Primary Games: Experiential Learning Activities for Teaching Children K-8*. San Francisco: Jossey-Bass, 2002. These 25 powerful games can be adapted for many instructional purposes.

Rime Pull-through Practice Cards

These sliders can be used to introduce or review rime families. They work well with regular paper or light card stock, but last longer and glide more smoothly if laminated.

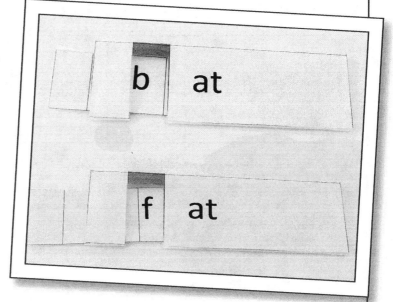

Figure 1: Photo of a Finished Slider

Materials

- sleeve pattern
- rime word lists
- stapler
- markers
- pull-through strip pattern

Optional: laminating equipment or stick-on transparent vinyl

Directions

1. Cut out the sample sleeve and fold along the dotted line.
2. Staple as indicated.
3. Cut out the shaded letter window.
4. Cut out the sample strip pattern.
5. Pull the strip through the sleeve, displaying one letter in the window at a time.
6. Use word lists to make sleeves and strips for other rime families.

A Two-Sided Rime Slider

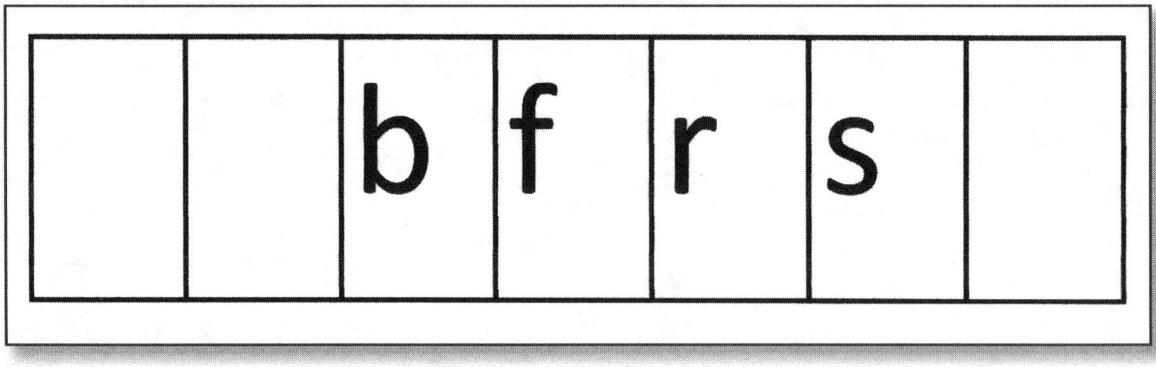

		b	f	r	s	

Figure 2 : A Two-Sided Slider Bar

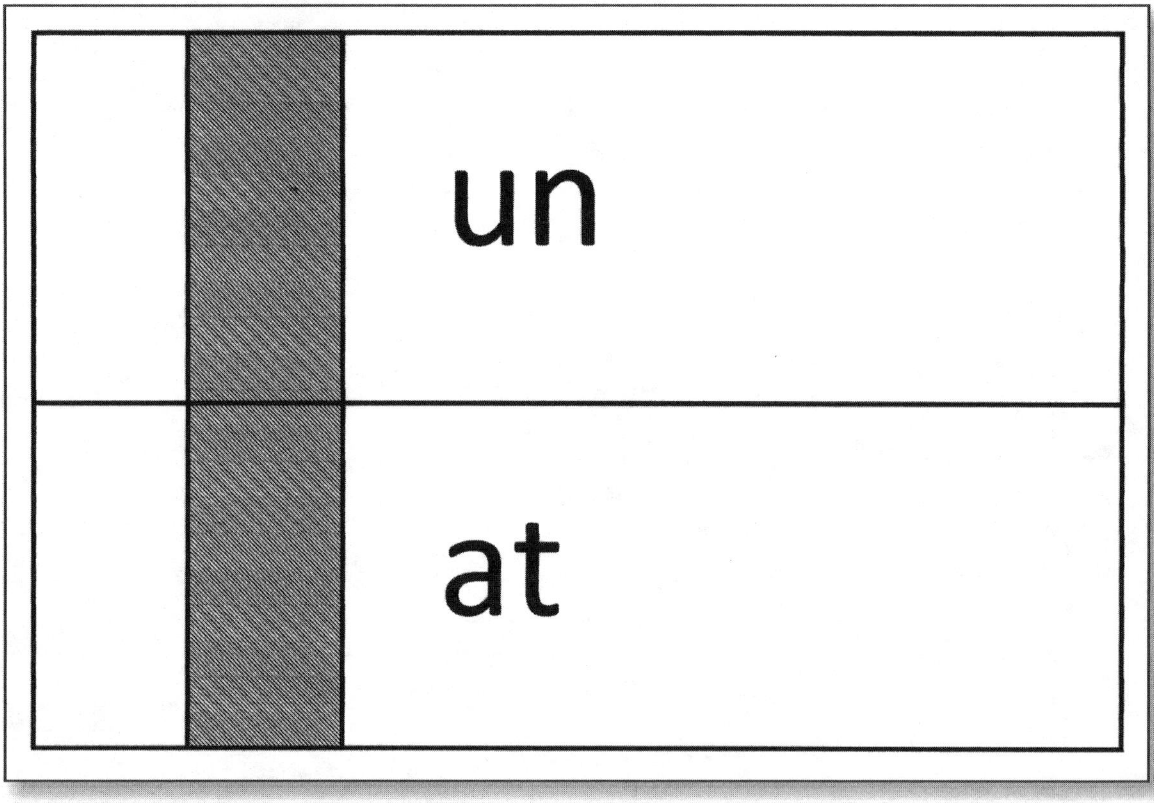

		un
		at

Figure 3: Pattern for a Two-Sided Slider Frame

Pattern for a One-Sided Slider

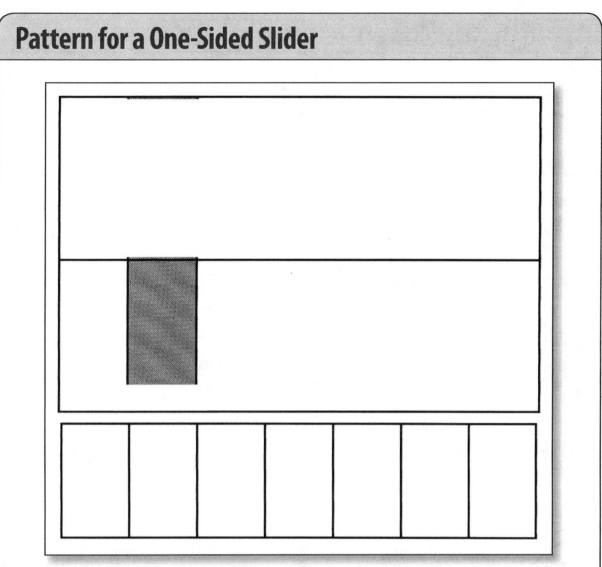

Figure 4: Pattern for a Blank, Single-Sided Slider

Most rimes have different initial letters, so double-sided sliders do not work. If used interchangeably, they create nonsense syllables and problematic words. Here is a blank slider and frame pattern. Use the suggested combinations below to create your own single-sided practice cards.

Suggested Letter and Ending Combinations

- ***all:*** b, c, f, h, m, t, w
- ***ash:*** b, c, d, h, m, r, s
- ***ell:*** b, d, f, n, s, t, w
- ***ill:*** b, d, j, f, h, p, s
- ***in:*** b, f, p, t, w
- ***ock:*** d, l, r, s, t
- ***op:*** b, h, m, p, t
- ***ump:*** b, d, l, p
- ***ace:*** f, l, p, r
- ***ime:*** d, l, r, t

- ***an:*** d, f, m, n, p, r, t
- ***ack:*** b, h, l, p, r, s, t
- ***est:*** b, n, p, r, t, w, z
- ***ing:*** k, d, p, r, s, w
- ***ink:*** l, m, p, r, s, w
- ***ot:*** d, g, c, h, l, n, p, r, t
- ***ug:*** b, d, h, j, l, m, r, t
- ***ain:*** g, m, p, r
- ***eed:*** d, f, s, w
- ***ine:*** d, f, l, m, n, p

- ***ap:*** c. g, l, m, n, r, s, t, z
- ***aw:*** c, l, p, r, s
- ***ick:*** l, p, s, t, w
- ***ip:*** d, h, l, s, t, z
- ***unk:*** ch, cl, d, s, h
- ***og:*** b, d, f, h, l
- ***uck:*** b, d, l, t
- ***ate:*** d, f, g, h, l, m, r
- ***eal:*** d, m, r, s
- ***one:*** b, l, t, z, ph

Introducing the Concept of Rime

"Rime Time" is the only verse that features more than one rime family. Each rime will have its own unique activity later in the book. The purpose of this ditty is to introduce the idea of a rime to young learners.

PRESENTING THE CONCEPT

- Introduce the verse by printing the words *name* and *game* on the board.
- Encourage students to name each letter as you point to it.
- Say each word. Example: "N-a-m-e, Name."
- Ask, "Name, game: what part's the same?"
- Challenge students to find the letters both words have in common.
- Explain that *name, game,* and *same* are rimes.
- Ask students to raise their hands if *fame* belongs to the same word family.
- Challenge them to do the same for *take, lame, lamb,* and *tame*.

PRESENTING THE VERSE

Next, introduce the verse. Slap your knees, clap your hands, and snap your fingers as you repeat the words in the second half of each line. Encourage the participants to join you. Then, write *clap, clap,* and *snap* on the board. Encourage students to notice which letters stay the same and which letters change.

   Repeat this cycle with every line. Then go through the entire verse without stopping, encouraging participants to join in for each refrain. It is fun to do these poems several times. Try them fast, then slow, or loud, then soft.

RIME TIME: AN ACTION VERSE

A rime for *slap* is *clap* or *snap: Slap, clap, snap.*

A rime for *say* is *day* or *hay: Say, day, hay.*

A rime for *sun* is *run* or *fun: Sun, run, fun.*

A rime for *hill* is *mill* or *will: Hill, mill, will.*

A rime for *fan* is *man* or *pan: Fan, man, pan.*

A rime for *name* is *same* or *game: Name, same, game.*

A rime for *hop* is *pop* or *stop: Hop, pop, STOP!*

Unit 1: The –*ack* Rime

PRESENTING THE VERSE

Write the words *Zack, Jack, Mack, back, pack,* and *sack* on the board or a chart. Help students to read the words, then invite them to notice which letters change and which do not. Encourage students to assemble their stick puppets. Invite them to follow along and work the puppets as you read the play.

On the second run-through, pause to let the children fill in the bold words. Advanced students may use copies of the script to produce the play in pairs or small groups. For a more elaborate presentation, puppeteers may crouch below a table, or two other students may hold up a piece of cloth.

Mack's Lost Pack: A Rime Mystery Play

Zack and Jack are looking at a banner that says "Zack and Jack, We Can Find It!"
> *Mack comes in.*

Mack: Are you **Zack**?

Zack: Yes, I'm **Zack**.

Mack: Are you **Jack**?

Jack: Yes, I'm **Jack**.

Mack: My name is **Mack**. I lost my **pack**. It is blue and red and **black**.

Zack: Do not worry.

Jack: We'll get it **back**.

Zack: We will find that missing **sack**.

Jack: Did you come straight home from school?

Mack: Yes, that's my mother's rule.

Zack: Whispers to Jack. They nod.

Zack: Wait right here.

Jack: We will be **back**.

> *(The Zack and Jack puppets leave. They come back with the Pack.)*

Zack: Is this your **pack**? It is blue and red and **black**.

Jack: It was on the bus bench, **Mack**.

Mack: Thank you! Thank you, **Zack** and **Jack**. I'm so glad to have it **back**.

Drinking Straw Puppets for Mack's Lost Pack

Figure 5: Finished Stick Puppets

Stick puppets are small and easy to make. They can be used with or without a stage. Patterns are provided here, but once children understand the size required, they can easily draw their own characters on ordinary paper, light cardboard, or construction paper.

Materials

- craft sticks
- copies of the patterns
- crayons or colored markers
- drinking straws or craft sticks
- scissors
- glue sticks or individual white glue dispensers

Directions

1. Assemble sample versions of the puppets before the session. Show them.
2. Separate participants into groups of four. (The pack is a puppet, too.)
3. Distribute the materials.
4. Encourage students to color each puppet differently. They should be recognizable as separate people.
5. Tell students to cut out the puppets along the lines.
6. Invite participants to attach a stick handle to each puppet.

Jack, Zack, and Mack Drinking Straw Puppet Patterns

Figure 6: Three Stick Puppet Patterns

SUGGESTED BOOKS TO COMPLETE THE PROGRAM

To create a complete program or lesson, add some or all of the following books:

Miss Nelson Is Back by Harry G. Allard

Click, Clack, Moo: Cows That Type by Doreen Cronin

Cock-A-Doodle Quack Quack by Ivor Baddiel

What's in Fox's Sack? An Old English Tale by Paul Galdone

Unit 2: The *—all* Rime

PRESENTING THE VERSE

Here's a story about an adventurous young mouse that lives in a toy store wall. First, introduce the words *small, wall, mall, ball, tall, fall, hall,* and *call*. Read the verse slowly. Pantomime a clue for the word *small* with your thumb and forefinger. Pause after the word *shop* to see if participants can guess the word *wall*. Encourage children to guess the other words in bold type.

Zall Hall, a Mouse in the Mall: An *—all* Verse

Zall Hall was very **small**. She lived inside a toy shop **wall**.

The shop was in a busy **mall**. Her door was near a yellow **ball**.

Which was wide as it was **tall**. Every night store gates would **fall**

And **Zall** crept out into the **mall**.

When morning came, her mom would **call**, "**Zall Hall, Zall Hall**!

Come back to the door behind the **ball**. **Zall Hall, Zall Hall**!

Come back to our home inside the **wall**."

Tall and Small: An –all Coloring Project

This simple craft reviews ideas of size and comparison while reminding students about the –all rime family.

Materials
- giraffe and mouse samples
- patterns
- markers or crayons
- scissors

Figure 7: Photo of a Finished Fold Giraffe and Fold Mouse

Directions
1. Show your samples.
2. Discuss the words *tall* and *small*. Ask for examples of things that are tall and things that are small.
3. Distribute copies of the pattern page.
4. Encourage participants to color the giraffe and the mouse.
5. Invite children to cut out each animal on the dotted lines.
6. Demonstrate how to fold each animal so it will stand up on its own.
7. Encourage participants to share the words printed on the picture with friends and relatives at home.

Tall and Small Coloring Project Pattern

tall
ball
call
fall
hall
mall
small

Fold on the line.

Figure 8: Patterns for a Tall Giraffe and a Small Mouse

Fold the pattern in half to stand on a table.

Call Ball: A Rime Family Game

This game can be used outdoors with a ball or indoors with a beanbag. In this lesson, the "Call Ball" game reviews –*all* rimes, but it can be used for any word family.

Materials
■ a bean bag or playground ball for each group of players

Directions
1. Divide participants into groups of five or six. Rehearse the verse and explain the rules.
2. The first player says, "Call ball, call ball. It's my turn and I say tall" (or any other –*all* word).
3. He rolls the ball or tosses the beanbag to any other player.
4. The catcher says, "Call ball, call ball. It's my turn, and I say (any other member of the same rime family except the one the player just before said.) For example, he might answer "Call ball, call ball. It's my turn and I say fall."
5. The catcher rolls or tosses the beanbag or ball to someone else, and the verse repeats.

SUGGESTED BOOKS TO COMPLETE THE PROGRAM

Milo Mouse and the Scary Monster by Louis Baum
Time Stops for No Mouse by Michael Hoeye

Unit 3: The –*an* Rime

PRESENTING THE VERSE

Introduce the words *can, Dan, fan, man, Nan, pan, ran,* and *tan*. Say that you will need help to tell this story. The first time you read the verse, pause to allow children time to fill in the words printed in bold. Read the verse again and challenge listeners to fill in all of the –*an* rime family words, including the characters' names.

Old Nan and Old Dan: An –*an* Verse

A tiny old man named **Dan** had a tiny old wife named **Nan**.

They lived in a rusty tin **can** beside an old frying **pan**.

They didn't have a car. They didn't have a **van**.

They didn't have any heat, and they didn't have a **fan**.

But inside the walls of that rusty old **can**

Old **Nan** had old **Dan** and **Dan** had old **Nan**.

Nan's Fan: An –*an* Project to Color and Fold

Children will review –*an* words as they color and fold this fan.

Materials
- patterns
- scissors
- paper clips
- markers

Directions
1. Review the words printed on the fan.
2. Color the fan.
3. Complete it with accordion folds along the lines.
4. Fold up the bottom on the line and fasten it with a paper clip.

Figure 9: Photo of the Finished Fan

Nan's Fan Pattern

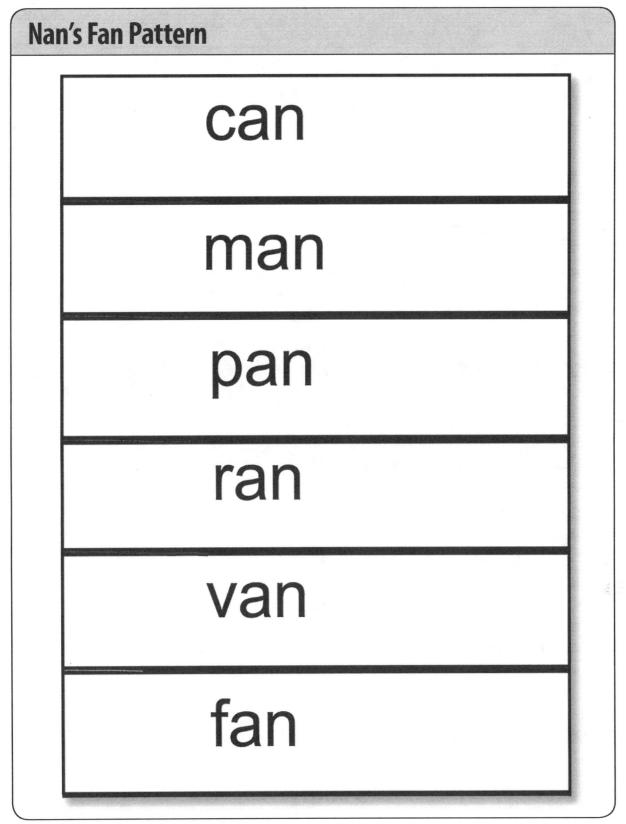

Figure 10: Nan's Fan Pattern

SUGGESTED BOOKS TO COMPLETE THE PROGRAM

For a complete story hour, add the classic story *The Gingerbread Man*, which features the same sounds, and a picture book about a quirky old couple, such as *Millions of Cats* by Wanda Gag.

Unit 4: The *–ap* Rime

PRESENTING THE VERSE

Use a chart, the board, or word cards to introduce the *–ap* rime words, which include *cap, flap, gap, lap, nap, rap, sap, trap,* and *tap*. If desired, draw or paste a picture of a baseball cap on the outside of a mailing envelope and place the word cards inside.

Tony and the Rap-Tap-Snap-Slap-Beat and Flap: An Action Verse

Tony could not take a nap, take a nap, take a nap.

(Action: put your palms together and lay your head on them, pretending to sleep.)

Tony could not take a nap; he heard a monster growling.

He heard its big wings beat and flap, beat and flap, beat and flap.

(Action: flap your hands to suggest flying.)

He heard its big wings beat and flap; he heard the monster flying.

He heard its sharp teeth grind and snap, grind and snap, grind and snap.

(Action: hold the heels of your palms together and snap your hands like jaws.)

He heard its sharp teeth grind and snap; he heard the monster munching.

He heard its claws rap and tap, rap and tap, rap and tap.

(Action: tap your fingertips against your lap.)

He heard its claws rap and tap; he heard the monster scratching.

He heard its long tail drag and slap, drag and slap, drag and slap.

(Action: put your palms together to make a monster tail and move it back and forth.)

He heard its long tail drag and slap; he heard the monster pacing.

Tony put on his hunting cap, his hunting cap, his hunting cap.

(Action: pretend to put on a brimmed cap.)

Tony put on his hunting cap; he was tired of waiting.

Tony and the Rap-Tap-Snap-Slap-Beat and Flap: An Action Verse (continued)

He tiptoed toward the snap and slap, the rap and tap, the beat and flap.

(Action: walk your hands, one at a time, across your lap.)

He crept down the hall so carefully that he was barely breathing.

He opened the door to the snap and slap, the rap and tap, the beat and flap.

(Action: pretend to open a door.)

He opened the door to the monster's lair and found . . . his sister smiling!

(Action: Smile!)

Fold a Flap: A Color, Cut, and Fold Project

Pictures can change just as words do. Here is a picture that changes with a simple fold. Review the word flap and its rime family before starting the craft. If desired, share a picture book with a folding flap format such as *Look Out, He's Behind You!* by Tony Bradman, or *Who's Laughing?* by David Bedford.

Figure 11: Photo of the Finished Flap Picture

Materials
■ sample flap picture
■ pattern
■ markers

Directions
1. Show the sample flap picture.
2. Distribute materials.
3. Encourage children to color the picture.
4. Help participants fold the page in half along the dark line.
5. Demonstrate how to fold the resulting strip along the dotted line.
6. Enjoy watching the monster change into a toddler standing up in her crib.

Fold a Flap Picture Pattern

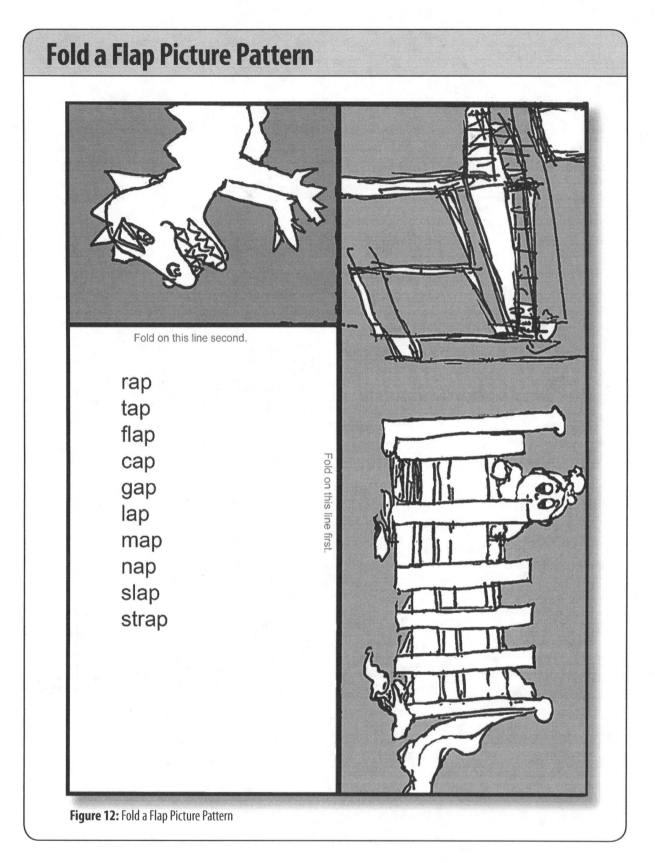

Fold on this line second.

rap
tap
flap
cap
gap
lap
map
nap
slap
strap

Fold on this line first.

Figure 12: Fold a Flap Picture Pattern

SUGGESTED BOOKS TO COMPLETE THE PROGRAM

Caps for Sale: A Tale of a Peddler, Some Monkeys and Their Monkey Business by Esphyr Slobodkina

Flap Your Wings by P.D. Eastman

Rap a Tap Tap by Diane Dillon and Leo Dillon

Unit 5: The —*at* Rime

PRESENTING THE VERSE

Write *at* on the board, read it aloud and encourage the children to repeat the sound after you.
Add letters, one at a time, to the beginning of the rime ending to create the following words: *cat, hat, brat, mat, rat,* and *sat.* Introduce the verse "It Isn't a Cat; It Isn't a Bat."

It Isn't a Cat; It Isn't a Bat: A Riddle Verse

What has ears, eats bugs, and flies at night? It isn't a cat. It isn't a hat. It's a _____ (bat)

What do you lie on in exercise class? It isn't a brat. It isn't a rat. It's a _____ (mat)

What should you wear on a hot, sunny day? It isn't a bat. It isn't a mat. It's a _____ (hat)

What eats tuna and purrs? It isn't a pat. It isn't a rat. It's a _____ (cat)

Cat Hat: A Color, Cut, and Fold Project to Wear

Materials
- sample hat
- scissors
- stapler
- hat pattern
- glue sticks

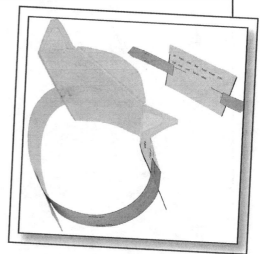

Figure 13: Photo of a Finished Cat Hat

Directions
1. Review the words *bat, brat, cat, fat, hat, mat, Nat, pat, rat, sat, slat,* and *tat.*
2. Display the sample hat.
3. Distribute materials.
4. Encourage students to color the hat pattern.
5. Tell students to cut out the parts along the lines.
6. Help students assemble the parts. The band is strongest when attached with a stapler.

Cat Hat Pattern

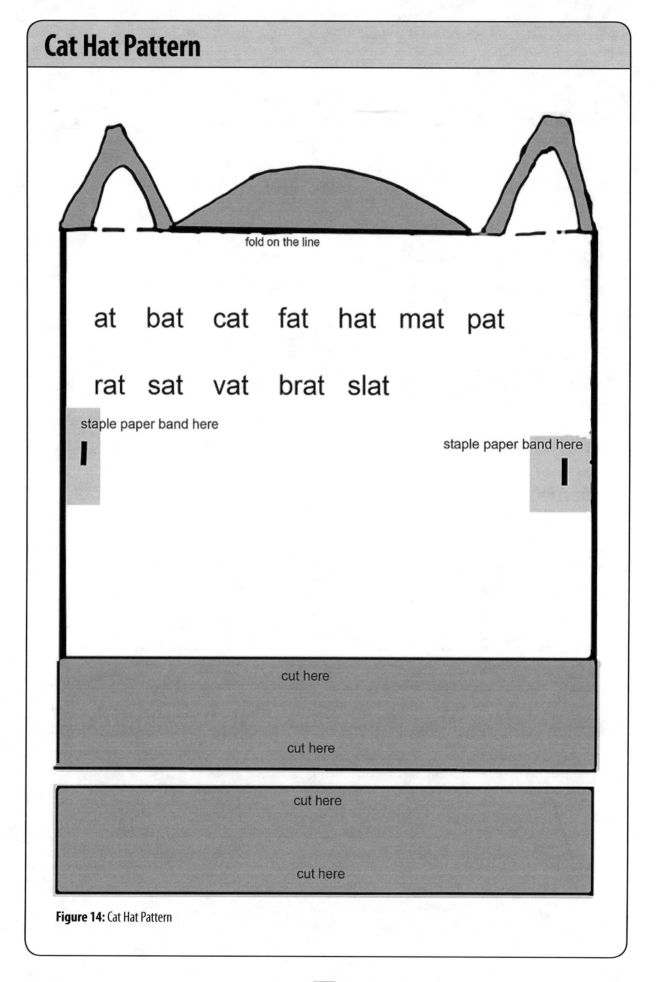

fold on the line

at bat cat fat hat mat pat

rat sat vat brat slat

staple paper band here

staple paper band here

cut here

cut here

cut here

cut here

Figure 14: Cat Hat Pattern

Split Splat, Pat That Cat: A Game

Here's a variation on a vintage dramatic play game that is sure to make everyone laugh. Use it on a rainy day or at the end of a long afternoon.

Materials
■ chairs

Directions
1. Invite all players to sit in a circle in chairs.
2. Review the *–at* words including *cat, mat, sat, hat, fat,* and *pat.*
3. Choose a player to be the first cat.
4. The cat must go to each player in the circle and meow three times, pretending to be a cat who wants to be petted. The cat should try to make the chosen victim laugh.
5. Each time the cat meows, the victim must say, "Split, splat, pat that cat" without laughing. If the seated player giggles, he and the cat trade places. If he does not laugh, the cat moves on to another player.
6. Traditionally, the cat crawls from player to player, and the victim pats the cat on the head. Some settings do not lend themselves to this. Use your own judgment.

SUGGESTED BOOKS TO COMPLETE THE PROGRAM

To create a memorable story hour, add a simple riddle book, such as *Hey Diddle Riddle, a Silly Nursery Rhyme Flap Book* by Wendi Silvano. Other related picture books include *The Fat Cat*, a Danish folktale by Jack Kent, and *The Cat in the Hat* by Dr. Seuss.

Unit 6: The *–ank* Rime

PRESENTING THE RIME

Write *–ank* on a chart. Read it aloud and encourage listeners to repeat the sound after you. Ask participants to think of words that end with that rime. Write the students' words on the chart. Possibilities include *bank, blank, Frank, plank, drank, prank, rank, sank, tank, thank, crank,* and *shrank.*

      Read the verse. At the end of each stanza, pause to allow students to guess the word. Show a prepared word card featuring the word, or write it on the chart as they guess. Encourage everyone to join in on the refrain, "Poor Frank!" or "Lucky Frank!"

Poor Frank, Lucky Frank: A Predictable Verse

There once was a book that was given to Frank. The cover was great,

but the pages were _____. (blank) Poor Frank! Poor Frank!

There once was a boat that was given to Frank.

All his friends sailed until the boat _____. (sank) Poor Frank! Poor Frank!

There once was a dollar that was given to Frank. He hurried downtown

to the savings _____. (bank) Lucky Frank! Lucky Frank!

There once was fish that was given to Frank. He took it right home

to his goldfish _____. (tank) Lucky Frank! Lucky Frank!

There once was some juice that was given to Frank.

He opened the carton, sat down, and _____ . (drank) Lucky Frank! Lucky Frank!

Thanks or No Thanks: An Activity

Review – *ank* rimes with this simple word card activity. It engages the entire group and provides instant feedback to students who are still uncertain about this skill. It also reviews rimes that have already been covered in previous lessons.

Materials

■ Word cards (large enough for the entire class to see). Each card should feature one of the following words: *bank, blank, Frank, plank, drank, prank, rank, sank, tank, thank, crank, shrank, back, bat, rack, rat, track, sat, tack, tap, slap,* and *nap*.

Directions

1. While shuffling the word cards, explain that you are going to show some cards. Instruct participants to read each card silently.
2. If the word on a card rhymes with *thank*, they should raise their hands (or stand up). If it does not rhyme with *thank*, they should shake their heads from side to side (or stay seated).
3. As the activity progresses, put the agreed-upon thank rhymes in one pile and the non-rimes in another.
4. At the end of the activity, hold up the cards one at a time and encourage students to read them aloud. Review the sounds of initial consonants or blends as needed.

Blank Frank: A Color and Cut Project

Frankenstein's monster. For maximum effect, read *Frank Was a Monster Who Wanted to Dance* by Keith Graves.

Figure 15: Photo of a Finished Frankenstein Monster Mask

Materials
- sample Frankenstein mask
- Blank Frank pattern
- glue
- green and purple crayons or markers
- scissors

Directions
1. Show the mask sample.
2. Encourage students to color the mask, adding imaginative features to make it scary.
3. Show them how to cut off the strip along the side of the page and glue the ends to each side.
4. For maximum creepiness, and safety, the mask is worn on the back of the head. Wearers slip it on like a backwards baseball cap with the paper band in the front.

SUGGESTED BOOKS TO COMPLETE THE PROGRAM

Fortunately by Remy Charlip

That's Good! That's Bad! by Margery Cuyler

Frank Was a Monster Who Wanted to Dance by Keith Graves

Figure 16: Blank Frank Pattern

Unit 7: The *—ash* Rime

PRESENTING THE VERSE

Bring a clean small trash can (wastebasket) with the following word cards buried under some crumpled papers: *smash, stash, crash, sash, cash, dash, flash,* and *rash*. They should be arranged so you can pull them out in order. There should be a large label on the can reading Trash. Pull the words out one at a time and hold them up as you present the verse.

Larry Dash Loves Trash: A Participation Verse

Larry Dash loves trash. He loves to mash it. He loves to smash it.

He loves to hear it bang and crash. Larry Dash loves trash.

Mash, smash, bash, crash, stinky, slimy, mushy trash!

Larry Dash loves trash. He loves tin cans and moldy hash.

He loves dried leaves, old wood, and ash. Larry Dash loves trash.

Mash, smash, bash, crash. Stinky, slimy, mushy trash!

Trash Truck: A Color and Fold Project

Review words that rhyme with trash. Discuss trash trucks and what would happen if they did not come each week to carry waste away to the city dump.

Materials
- sample trash truck
- trash truck patterns
- scissors
- crayons
- glue

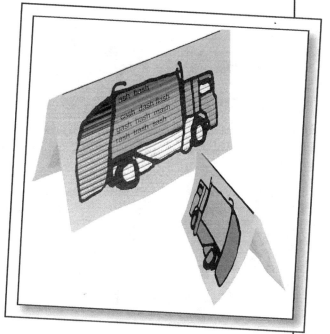

Figure 17: Photo of Finished Trash Trunk

Directions
1. Show students the sample truck.
2. Pass out the patterns and tell students to color the truck's top and sides.
3. Show students how to cut out the truck along the heavy lines.
4. Demonstrate how to fold the truck along the dashed lines.
5. Show students how to glue the truck's ends together.

SUGGESTED BOOKS TO COMPLETE THE PROGRAM

The Great Trash Bash by Loreen Leedy

Trash Trucks by Daniel Kirk

Smash! Mash! Crash! There Goes the Trash! by Barbara Odanaka

ash bash

cash dash flash
gash hash mash
rash trash sash

Figure 18: Trash Truck Pattern

Unit 8: The −*aw* Rime

PRESENTING THE VERSE

Discuss the fact that drawing is a skill like swimming or reading. The more you draw, the better you are at drawing. Introduce words that rhyme with *draw*. They include *saw, paw, raw, straw, law, claw,* and *flaw*. Use word cards or write them on a chart.

When Presenting the Verse, you should read the first stanza straight through to set up the pattern. Then, read it again, encouraging students to join in on the repeated phrases. Show word cards, or point to −*aw* rimes as you say them.

Sam and His Little Blue Sketchbook: A Participation Verse

A boy named Sam loved to *draw,* loved to *draw,* loved to *draw.*

A boy named Sam loved to *draw* in his little blue sketchbook.

He drew every detail that he *saw,* that he *saw,* that he *saw.*

He drew every detail that he *saw* in his little blue sketchbook.

He drew his kitten licking her *paw,* licking her *paw,* licking her *paw.*

He drew his kitten licking her *paw,* in his little blue sketchbook.

He drew his hamster sleeping in *straw,* sleeping in *straw,* sleeping in *straw.*

He drew his hamster sleeping in *straw* in his little blue sketchbook.

He drew his uncle studying *law,* studying *law,* studying *law.*

He drew his uncle studying *law* in his little blue sketchbook.

He drew a big crow saying *"caw!"* saying *"caw,"* saying *"caw."*

He drew a big crow saying *"caw"* in his little blue sketchbook.

Sam was a boy who loved to *draw,* loved to *draw,* loved to *draw.*

Sam was a boy who loved to *draw* in his little blue sketchbook.

My Little Blue Sketchbook: A Creative Project

Review the −*aw* rime. Ask students what Sam drew in his sketchbook. Ask participants what they would draw if they had a little blue sketchbook.

Materials
■ sample sketchbook
■ sketchbook patterns
■ pencils
■ blue crayons or markers

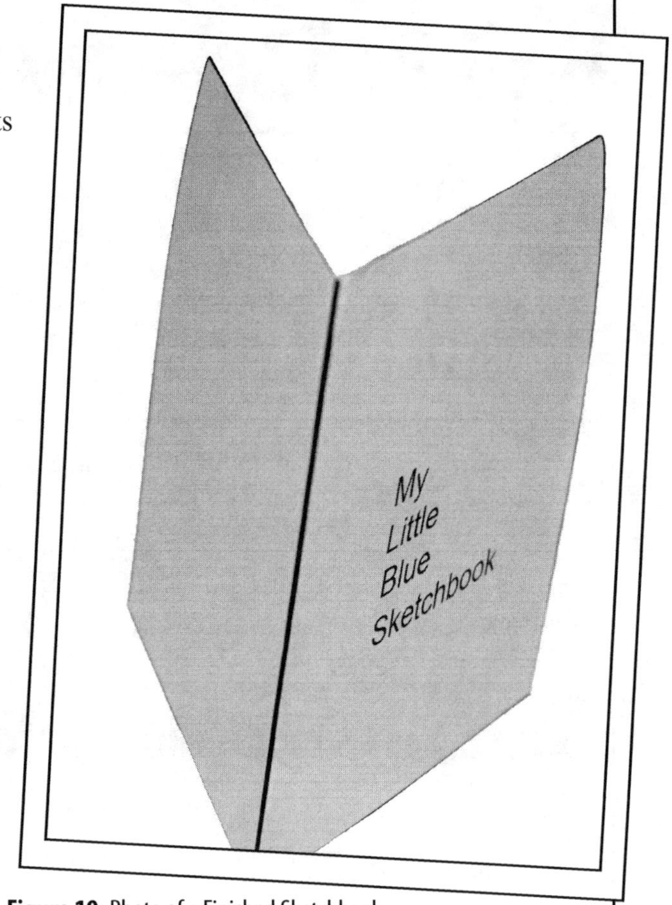

Figure 19: Photo of a Finished Sketchbook

Directions
1. Show the sample sketchbook.
2. Distribute the patterns.
3. Demonstrate how to fold the books on the lines.
4. Encourage students to color the front of their sketchbooks blue.
5. Invite them to do some drawings in their sketchbooks.
6. Offer each student a chance to talk about a drawing.

Little Blue Sketchbook Pattern

aw
caw
draw
flaw
law
paw
raw
saw

My
Little
Blue
Sketchbook

Figure 20: Little Blue Sketchbook Pattern

Caw, Caw, Caw, That's What I Saw! A Memory Activity

Play this easy variation on a classic memory game to improve observation and recall.

Materials
- a cafeteria tray
- 8-10 familiar items from the classroom that will fit on the tray such as a pencil, an eraser, a ruler, a paintbrush, a crayon, a paper clip, a penny, a roll of tape, a rubber band

Directions

1. Ask students what sound crows make. Point out that *caw* rhymes with *draw*. Write it on a chart or show a word card to emphasize the spelling of the rime.

2. Explain that crows like to find treasures and carry them away. Explain that, for the next few minutes, they are going to be crows.

3. Teach them the phrase "Caw, Caw, Caw, That's What I Saw!" Write it on the board or on a chart and encourage them to read it with you.

4. Tell the children that you are going to show them a tray with a lot of items on it, and you want them to remember everything they see.

5. Show them the tray for about a minute. Watch for restlessness.

6. Hide the tray.

7. Go around the circle, asking each participant, in turn, to name one thing that was on the tray.

8. If other students agree with the named item, they should say "Caw, caw, caw, that's what I saw!" Participants who do not agree should remain silent.

9. At the end of the session, show the tray again and ask participants to name any items that have been omitted.

SUGGESTED BOOKS TO COMPLETE THE PROGRAM

Draw Me a Star by Eric Carle

Selina and the Bear Paw Quilt by Barbara Smucker

When Agnes Caws by Candace Fleming

Unit 9: The –*ell* Rime

PRESENTING THE VERSE

Introduce the –*ell* rime. Make a well by wrapping a large coffee can or paint can in tan, gray, or brown construction paper. Use a marker to draw large rounded stones on the paper.

Make word cards featuring the –*ell* words in the verse in order. Pull out each card and show it at the appropriate moment in the presentation.

If you do not want to use a coffee can, draw a wishing well on the outside of a 9″ x 12″ manila mailing envelope. Put the cards in the envelope.

N-E-L-L: A Spell-It-Out Verse

Long ago a girl named Nell took a walk through Delly Dell.

N- E-L- L, Nell (Point to the letters on the card and encourage students to join you.)

D-E-L-L, Dell

She stopped to rest by a wishing well. Along came a man with things to sell.

W-E-L-L, well, S-E-L-L, sell

The man sold her a silver bell, and that is all I have to tell.

B-E-L- L, bell, T-E-L-L, tell

Wishing Well: A Color, Cut, and Tape Project

Review *–ell* words, especially the word *well*, with this simple activity.

Materials
- sample wishing well
- wishing well pattern
- scissors
- crayons or markers
- staplers or glue

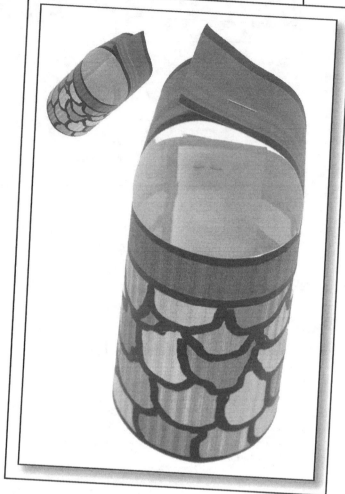

Figure 21: Photo of Finished Wishing Well

Directions
1. Discuss the idea of a wishing well. Invite students to share wishes they might make if there were a real wishing well outside.
2. Distribute the well patterns.
3. Encourage students to color in the wells and the coins.
4. Demonstrate how to cut out the well and the coins.
5. Help students staple the well together.
6. Encourage students to read the words printed on the coins to their friends and to relatives at home.

SUGGESTED BOOKS TO COMPLETE THE PROGRAM

You Can't Smell a Flower with Your Ear! by Joanna Cole

Junie B., First Grader: Jingle Bells, Batman Smells! (p.s. so does May.) by Barbara Park

The Farmer in the Dell by Pam Adams

The Night the Moon Fell: A Maya Myth by Pat Mora

Wishing Well Pattern

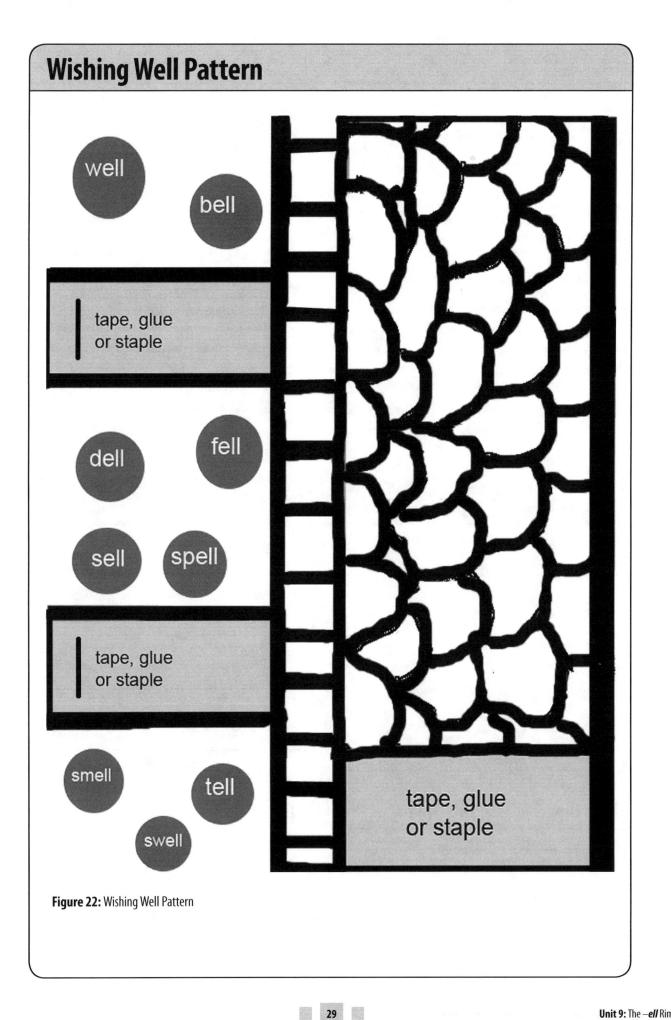

Figure 22: Wishing Well Pattern

Unit 10: The *–est* Rime

PRESENTING THE VERSE

Introduce *–est* words used in the verse. On a manila mailing envelope, draw a nest and write the word *nest*.

Cut out seven large egg shapes and print one of the words on each. Put them in the envelope. Pull out each egg and help children read the words. Cover up the initial consonant and repeat the *–ell* sound each time, then uncover the initial consonant, and say the word.

Read the verse, encouraging students to participate by joining in on the repeated refrain. If there is time, repeat the entire verse and invite students to join in by pausing before the *–est* words and holding up the word *eggs*.

Everything's Best Out in the West: A Whoopin' Fine Verse

Everything's *best* out in the *West*.

A bird is a bird and a *nest* is a *nest*. Yippee-kyo-ky-yeah!

Everything's *best* out in the *West*.

A pal is a pal and a *pest* is a *pest*. Yippee-kyo-ky-yeah!

Everything's *best* out in the *West*.

Work is work and *rest* is *rest*. Yippee-kyo-ky-yeah!

Everything's *best* out in the *West*.

Better is fine, but *best* is *best!* Yippee-kyo-ky-yeah!

SUGGESTED BOOKS TO COMPLETE THE PROGRAM

The Best Nest by P.D. Eastman

Way Out West Lives a Coyote Named Frank by Jillian Lund

First Grade Takes a Test by Miriam Cohen

Mother, You're the Best! (But Sister, You're a Pest!) by Diane Degroat

The Best Place for the Nest: A Play for Two Birds

Father Bird: This roof is the best place for our nest.

Mother Bird: I am not sure. It is too close to the road. It will be noisy.

Father Bird: You are right. I have another idea. Come on. (They fly away.)

   (Father Bird and Mother Bird come back in.)

Father Bird: This tree is the best place for our nest.

Mother Bird: I am not sure. It is too windy. It will be cold.

Father Bird: You are right. I have another idea. Come on. (They fly away.)

Father Bird: (Comes in alone.) This porch is the best place for our nest.

Mother Bird: (Off stage.) I hope this spot is really the best.

Father Bird: Hurry. I am sure this spot will pass your test. It is the best place for our nest.

Mother Bird: (Comes in. Looks around.) It is much better than the rest. It is the best place for our nest.

Bird Puppets: A Color, Cut, and Tape Project

With these two bird puppets, each child can act out the play.

Materials
- sample bird puppets
- markers
- copies of the play
- bird patterns
- scissors

Figure 23: Photo of Finished Bird Puppets

Directions

1. Introduce the play. Read it through as children follow along. Tell participants they will be making puppets to act it out. Show them the sample bird puppets.
2. Distribute the bird puppet pattern page.
3. Encourage students to color the birds and cut them out.
4. Glue or staple the bands on each puppet to form a loop as shown.
5. Read the play again, encouraging participants to act it out with their puppets.
6. Invite students to choose partners and act out the play together. They may use the script, perform the play from memory, or make up their own words.

Bird Puppets Pattern

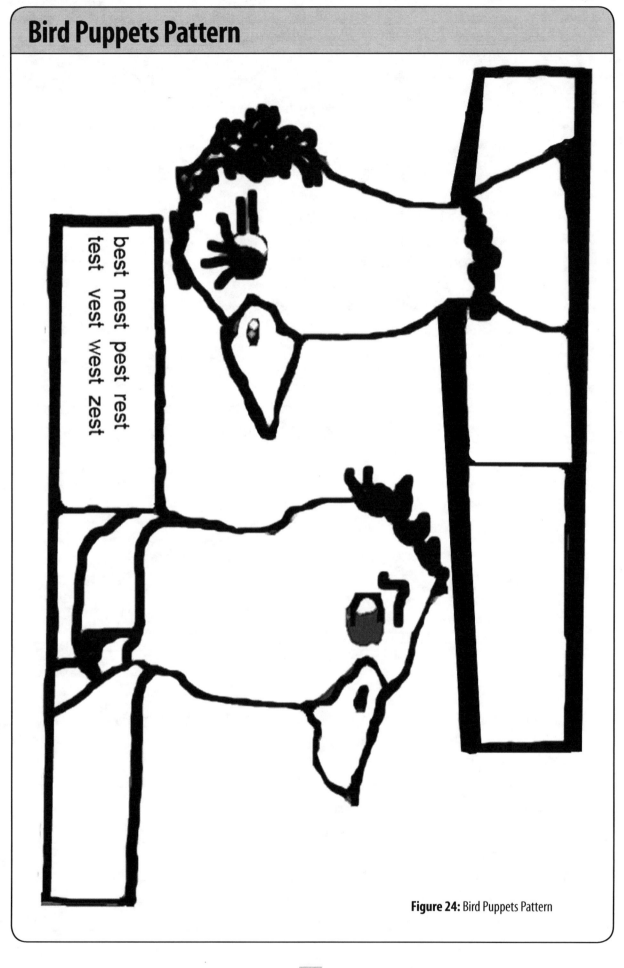

best nest pest rest
test vest west zest

Figure 24: Bird Puppets Pattern

Unit 11: The *-ick* Rime

PRESENTING THE VERSE

Introduce the *–ick* words. They include *flick, lick, pick, sick, tick, wick, stick, brick, trick,* and *slick*. Present the verse and invite students to join in. Encourage participants to pretend they are holding an imaginary stick that can transform itself with a wish.

A Trick Stick: An Imagination Participation Verse

Leader: This is really a trick stick.

Boys: This is really a trick stick. **Girls:** This is really a trick stick.

Leader: It can be a candle wick lighting the way in the dark. (Pretend to hold a candle.)

Leader: This is really a trick stick.

Boys: This is really a trick stick. **Girls:** This is really a trick stick.

Leader: It can be a guitar pick playing a song in the park. (Play the air guitar.)

Leader: This is really a trick stick.

Boys: This is really a trick stick. **Girls:** This is really a trick stick.

Leader: It can make a clock tick keeping time in the hall. (Put your palms together and move your hands side to side like a pendulum.)

Leader: This is really a lollipop stick.

Boys: This is really a lollipop stick. **Girls:** This is really a lollipop stick.

Leader: I'll lick, and lick, and lick, until I have eaten it all! (Pretend to lick a lollipop.)

Quick Tricks: A Pantomime Activity

Materials
■ *Cat Tricks* by Keith Baker

Directions
1. Read the story aloud and review the cat's tricks.
2. Divide participants into groups of three.
3. Invite each participant to think of a simple activity to act out.
4. Tell students to take turns pantomiming their chosen activity. Others in their group should try to guess what they are doing.

A Trick Stick: A Color, Roll, and Tape Project

Materials
■ sample Trick Stick
■ Trick Stick pattern
■ markers
■ transparent tape

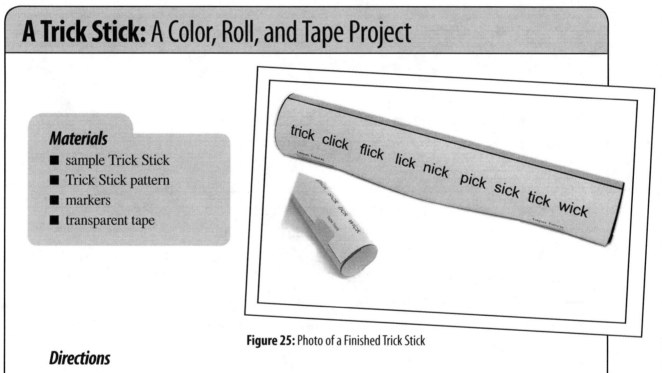

Figure 25: Photo of a Finished Trick Stick

Directions
1. Distribute the Trick Stick patterns.
2. Help children read the *–ick* words on the stick.
3. Show the sample stick.
4. Encourage children to color the designs on the stick.
5. Demonstrate how to roll the stick.
6. Tape the stick so it stays rolled.

Trick Stick Pattern

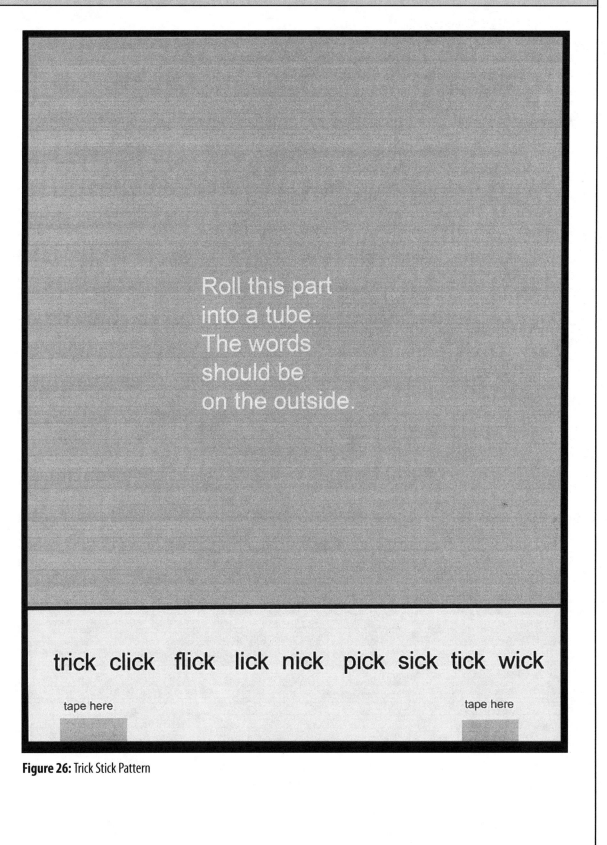

Roll this part into a tube. The words should be on the outside.

trick click flick lick nick pick sick tick wick

tape here

tape here

Figure 26: Trick Stick Pattern

SUGGESTED BOOKS TO COMPLETE THE PROGRAM

When Daddy's Truck Picks Me Up by Jana Novotny Hunter

I Can Lick 30 Tigers Today! and Other Stories by Dr. Seuss

Dick Whittington and His Cat by Marcia Brown

Bear Feels Sick by Karma Wilson

Stick by Steve Breen

Mother, Mother, I Feel Sick; Send for the Doctor, Quick, Quick, Quick by Remy Charlip

Unit 12: The *–ill* Rime

PRESENTING THE VERSE

Use your Bill and Will sample puppets to introduce the *–ill* words. The rimes include *Bill, Jill, fill, hill, pill, still, will, mill, quill, spill, thrill,* and *drill.* If you wish, the two puppets can introduce themselves, and then take turns reading the words off a chart, off the board, or off word cards.

Encourage children to recite "Jack and Jill." Ask why the children in the traditional nursery rhyme had to carry water in a pail instead of just turning on a faucet. If necessary, explain that things are different now than they were 200 years ago.

Tell participants that the verse they are going to hear is about what might have happened the day after Jack and Jill fell down. Read the verse, encouraging students to join in on the refrain, pointing to each *–ill* word, or holding up a word card as it appears in the rhyme.

Jack's Invitation to Jill: A Pattern Verse

I'm feeling fine, how are you, Jill, how are you Jill, how are you Jill?

I'm feeling fine, how are you Jill, early this bright morning?

Will you come with me up the hill, up the hill, up the hill?

Will you come with me up the hill, early in this bright morning?

The stream is running by the mill, by the mill, by the mill.

The stream is running by the mill early this bright morning.

And, Jill, we have a pail to fill, pail to fill, pail to fill.

And, Jill, we have a pail to fill early this bright morning.

We can't let the water spill, water spill, water spill.

We can't let the water spill early this bright morning.

The sun is up. Let's hurry, Jill, hurry Jill, hurry Jill!

The sun is up. Let's hurry, Jill, early this bright morning.

Bill and Will: A Riddle Play

Bill: It starts with an h and rhymes with fill. You can climb on it. What is it?

Will: Uh, is it a mill?

Bill: No, no, no! It starts with an h.

Will: Is it a hall?

Bill: No, no, no! It rhymes with fill.

Will: Is it a drill?

Bill: No, no, no! You can climb on it.

Will: Is it a rope?

Bill: No, no, no! It starts with an h. It rhymes with fill. You can climb on it. What is it?

Will: Hmm. It starts with an h. It rhymes with fill. That's h-ill. You can climb on it. Oh! It is a hill!

Bill: Yes, yes, yes! You are right! It is a hill. I knew you could do it!

SUGGESTED BOOKS TO COMPLETE THE PROGRAM

Mole's Hill: A Woodland Tale by Lois Ehlert

Will I Have a Friend? by Miriam Cohen

The Stars Will Still Shine by Cynthia Rylant

Jack and Jill and Big Dog Bill: A Phonics Reader by Martha Weston

Bill and Will Puppets: A Color, Cut, and Tape Project

Children will use these puppets to act out "Bill and Will: A Riddle Play."

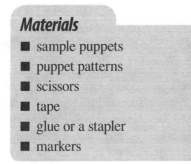

Materials
- sample puppets
- puppet patterns
- scissors
- tape
- glue or a stapler
- markers

Figure 27: Photo of the Finished Bill and Will Puppets

Directions

1. Distribute copies of the play. Read it through as the children follow along. Emphasize each of the *–ill* rimes.
2. Divide the group in half, assigning Bill's part to one group and Will's part to the others. Help each group read its part in turn.
3. Distribute the puppet patterns.
4. Encourage students to color the characters.
5. Demonstrate how to cut out and assemble the puppets. Show the sample puppets.
6. Invite students to cut out their puppets.
7. Help participants tape, glue, or staple the back bands in place.
8. Demonstrate how to act out the play.
9. Allow time for students to select partners and act out the play.
10. Encourage participants to act out the play at home.

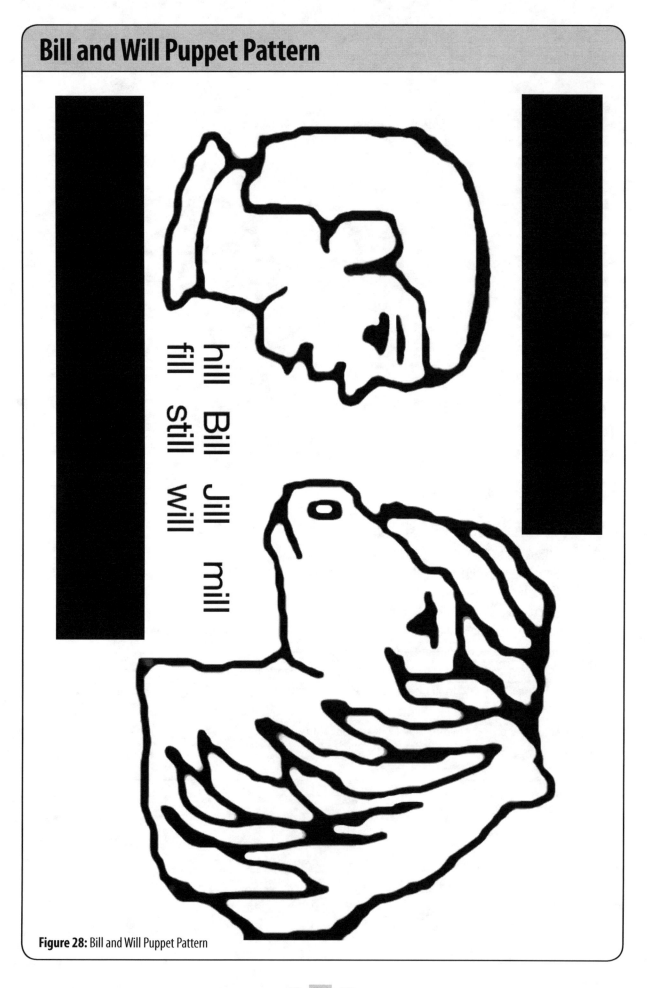

hill Bill Jill mill
fill still will

Figure 28: Bill and Will Puppet Pattern

Unit 13: The *–ing* Rime

PRESENTING THE VERSE

Use word cards, a chart, or the board to introduce the *–ing* words. They include *spring, sing, swing, wing, string, ring,* and *thing.* Discuss how bird parents build nests in the spring, care for their eggs, and feed their young.

This rhyme follows a very old form. It is a ballad, which means it is a poem that tells a story. Read the verse aloud, encouraging students to join in on each refrain. Read it a second time, holding up the word card and pausing for each *–ing* word.

One Day in Early Spring: A Birdie Ballad

One bright day in early spring, ding, ding, a derry-oh,

There was a bird who could not sing, ring-a, ling-a day.

He had a lady love named Ming, ding, ding, a derry-oh,

She was sweet and fair of wing, ring-a, ling-a day.

He brought her worms. He brought her string, ding, ding, a derry-oh,

He even brought a silver ring, ring-a, ling-a day.

She took the worms. She took the string, ding, ding, a derry-oh,

She took his love and silver ring, ring-a, ling-a day.

But then she asked for one more thing, ding, ding, a derry-oh,

She wanted him to stand and sing, ring-a, ling-a day.

He opened his beak and thought of Ming, ding, ding, a derry-oh,

Then, all at once, he could sing! Ring-a, ling-a day.

They built a nest from sticks and string, ding, ding, a derry-oh,

and raised a family near the swing, ring-a, ling-a day.

Singer with Wings: A Color, Cut, and Fold Project

Review the *–ing* rime before presenting this craft project. Remind students that many birds can sing and that most birds can also fly. Ask what birds have that allow them to fly. Say that it starts with a *w* and rhymes with *sing*.

Materials
- sample flying bird
- fold-over bird pattern sheets
- scissors
- markers (wax in crayons will make the bird too heavy)

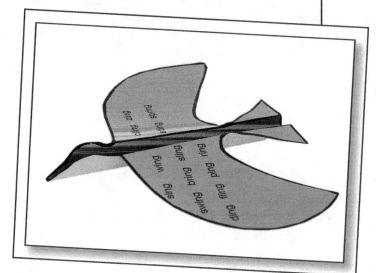

Figure 29: Photo of the Flying Bird

Directions
1. Show the sample flying bird.
2. Distribute the pattern sheets. Invite students to color the bird.
3. Tell students to cut out the bird.
4. Demonstrate how to fold the bird. Show how to hold it underneath and move it up and down to make its wings flap. Don't worry, if tossed, it will not fly far. It will just flutter down to the ground.
5. *Optional:* Demonstrate how to hold the fold lightly between your lips and hum to create a kazoo-like effect. Hint: Hold the bird at the head and tail for maximum vibration.

Fold-over Bird Pattern

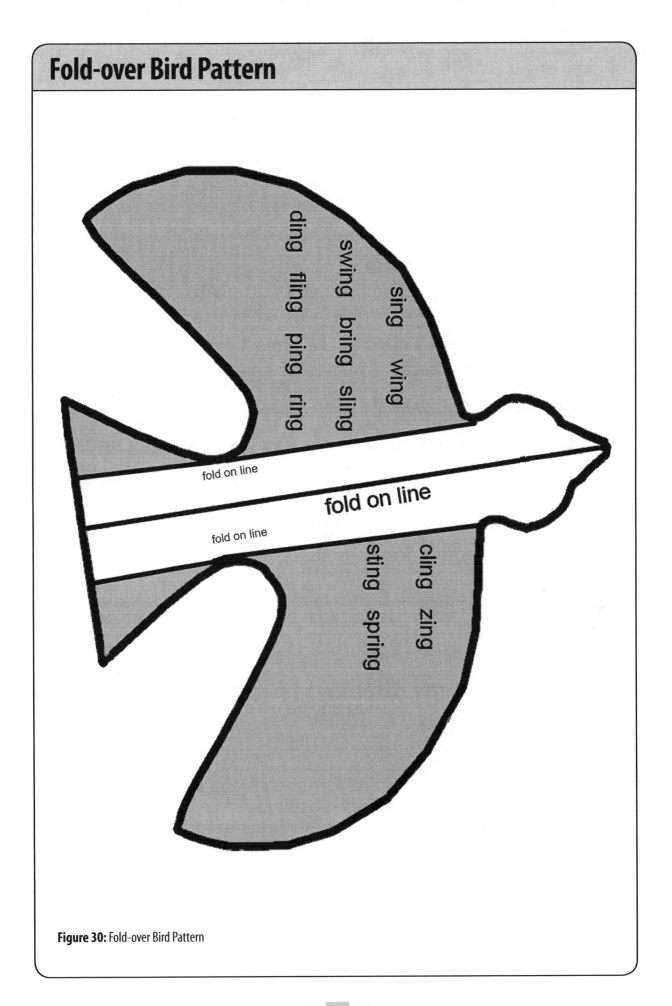

ding fling ping ring

swing bring sling

sing wing

fold on line

fold on line

fold on line

cling zing

sting spring

Figure 30: Fold-over Bird Pattern

What Will You Bring? A Listening and Remembering Activity

Materials
■ chairs

Directions

1. Seat children in a circle. Discuss what a picnic is and allow children to discuss memorable outdoor meals. Ask what sorts of things they might take to a picnic.
2. Use word cards to review the –*ing* rimes *bring, thing,* and *spring*. Ask students if they remember any other –*ing* rimes.
3. Explain that they are going to play a game. The object of the game is to listen carefully and to remember what they hear.
4. Say, "I'm going on a picnic this spring, and I am going to bring a basket."
5. Encourage students to repeat after you.
6. Invite the child next to you to name something else you might bring, such as a water jug.
7. Encourage students to join you as you say "I'm going on a picnic this spring and I am going to bring a basket and a water jug."
8. Continue around the circle until every child has contributed something different to the picnic.
9. Eventually, children will be able to play this without your help.

Note: More advanced students may want to play a more difficult version. Instead of adding anything that is sensible to the picnic, they should add only words that start with a certain consonant, such as *s* or *t*.

SUGGESTED BOOKS TO COMPLETE THE PROGRAM

Flap Your Wings by P.D. Eastman

The Wing on a Flea by Ed Emberley

The Wing Shop by Elvira Woodruff

Tico and the Golden Wings by Leo Lionni

Sing, Sophie! by Dayle Ann Dodds

Unit 14: The *–ip* Rime

PRESENTING THE VERSE

Introduce the *–ip* words in the verse. They include *dip, drip, flip, lip, sip, ship, whip, vip, zip, hip,* and *slip.*

Use a chart, the board, or word cards to display the words. If desired, draw or paste a picture of a family car or van on a mailing envelope. Include suitcases on top of the car to suggest a road trip. Place the word cards inside.

Invite students to discuss family trips. Explain that this verse is about a family's vacation at a resort. They will stay in a motel with a swimming pool. It could be in the mountains, in the desert, or at the beach. Present the verse, encouraging students to join in on each refrain. Hold up or point to the repeated *–ip* word as students say it.

Our Summer Trip: A Participation Verse

Last year we took a summer trip, a trip, a trip; we took a trip!

In the pool we took a dip, a dip, a dip; we took a dip.

My sister did a double flip, a flip, a flip; she did a flip.

We hung our wet trunks up to drip, to drip, to drip; we let them drip.

We saw a show at Rancho Zip, at Zip, at Zip; at Rancho Zip.

We watched a cowboy crack a whip, a whip, a whip; he cracked a whip.

We went to a lake called Percy Pip, Lake Pip, Lake Pip; Lake Percy Pip.

And there we sailed a model ship, a ship, a ship; a model ship.

My brother slipped and bit his lip, his lip, his lip; he bit his lip.

And that was the end of our summer trip, our trip, our trip; our summer trip.

Talking Lips: A Color, Cut, and Fold Project

These silly talking lips will help participants remember –*ip* rimes forever!

Materials

■ sample Talking Lips
■ Talking Lips pattern
■ scissors
■ markers
■ staplers or tape

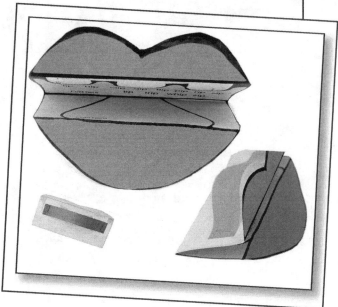

Figure 31: Photo of Finished Talking Lips

Directions

1. Show the Talking Lips sample. Demonstrate how it "talks." Make it say the –*ip* words.
2. Distribute the patterns and markers.
3. Encourage students to color the lips.
4. Demonstrate how to cut out the lips and the finger-holder strip. Distribute scissors.
5. Demonstrate how to fold the lips.
6. Help students attach the finger-holder strip.
7. Encourage students to make their lips say the –*ip* rhymes.

SUGGESTED BOOKS TO COMPLETE THE PROGRAM

D.W. Flips by Marc Brown

Drip, Drop by Sarah Weeks

Loud Lips Lucy by Tolya L. Thompson

The Trip by Ezra Jack Keats

Tip Tip Dig Dig by Emma Garcia

Sheep on a Ship by Nancy E. Shaw

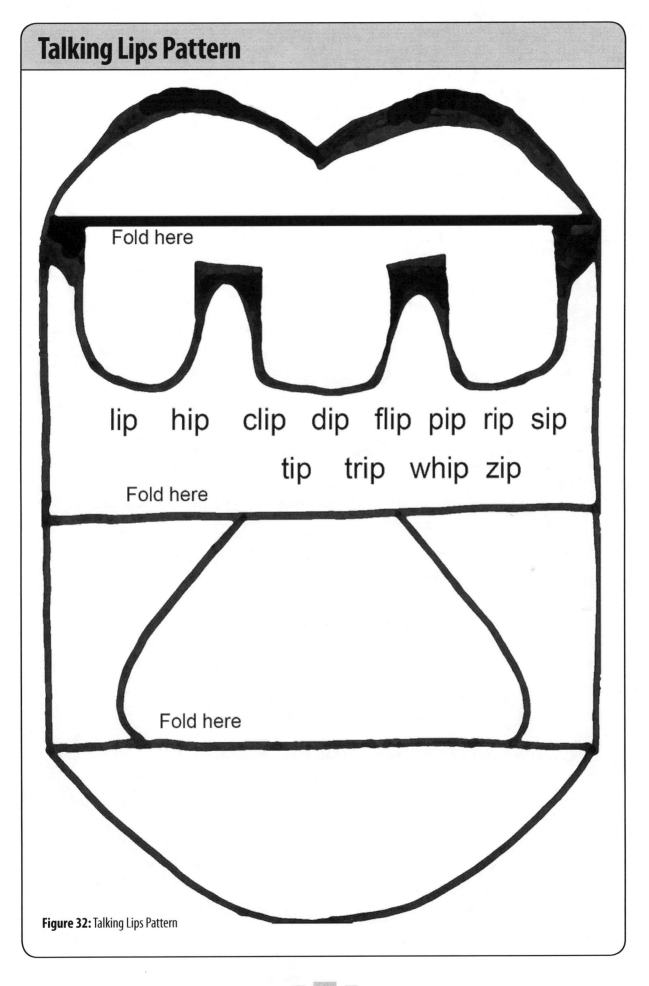

lip   hip   clip   dip   flip   pip   rip   sip

tip   trip   whip   zip

Figure 32: Talking Lips Pattern

Unit 15: The –*in* Rime

PRESENTING THE VERSE

Use a chart, the board, or word cards to introduce the –*in* words. They include *bin, chin, thin, fin, pin, tin, win, twin,* and *spin*. If desired, place the word cards in a plastic vegetable bin with the word *bin* written on the side.

Tell participants you are going to need their help with this verse. Rehearse the refrain "Put your hands out. Pull them back in. Here's a game we all can win." Then, read the verse slowly, encouraging children to join you in the actions. Repeat the entire rhyme, pausing to allow learners to fill in the –*in* words.

Tug Your Ears and Tap Your Chin: An Action Verse

Tug your ears. (Pull on your ears gently.)

Tap your chin. (Tap your chin with both index fingers.)

Put your hands out. (Put both hands out in front of you.)

Pull 'em back in. (Put both hands on your chest.)

Here's a game we all can win. (On the word win, lift both arms above your head as if cheering.)

Cover your eyes. Tap your chin. Put your hands out. Pull 'em back in.

Here's a game we all can win.

Pinch your nose. Tap your chin. Put your hands out. Pull 'em back in.

Here's a game we all can win.

Frown a frown. Grin a grin. Put your hands out. Pull 'em back in.

Here's a game we all can win.

Award Ribbon Bookmark: A Color and Cut Project

Everyone wants to win a blue ribbon. Here's one that doubles as a bookmark, after the glue dries.

Materials
- sample bookmark
- bookmark pattern page
- scissors
- glue sticks
- pencils

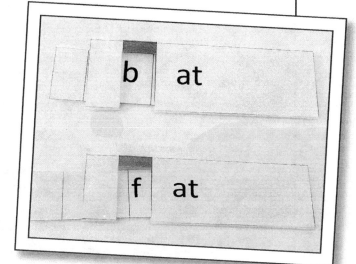

Figure 33: Photo of a Finished Bookmark

Directions

1. Ask participants about prizes they have won. Explain that today, everyone will take home an award. Show the sample bookmark.
2. Distribute the pattern pages.
3. Encourage students to cut out the ribbon on the solid lines.
4. Show students how to fold the award on the dotted lines.
5. Demonstrate how to glue or tape the two halves of the award together.
6. Help children print their names on the line.
7. *Optional:* Help children apply gold seals or stars to the reverse side of the award.
8. Encourage students to read the *–in* words printed on the award to their parents at home.

SUGGESTED BOOKS TO COMPLETE THE PROGRAM

The Twiddle Twins' Haunted House by Howard Goldsmith

The Tin Forest by Helen Ward

Alfie Wins a Prize by Shirley Hughes

Splashy Fins, Flashy Skin, Deep Sea Rhymes to Make You Grin by Cynthia Copeland

Award Ribbon Bookmark Pattern

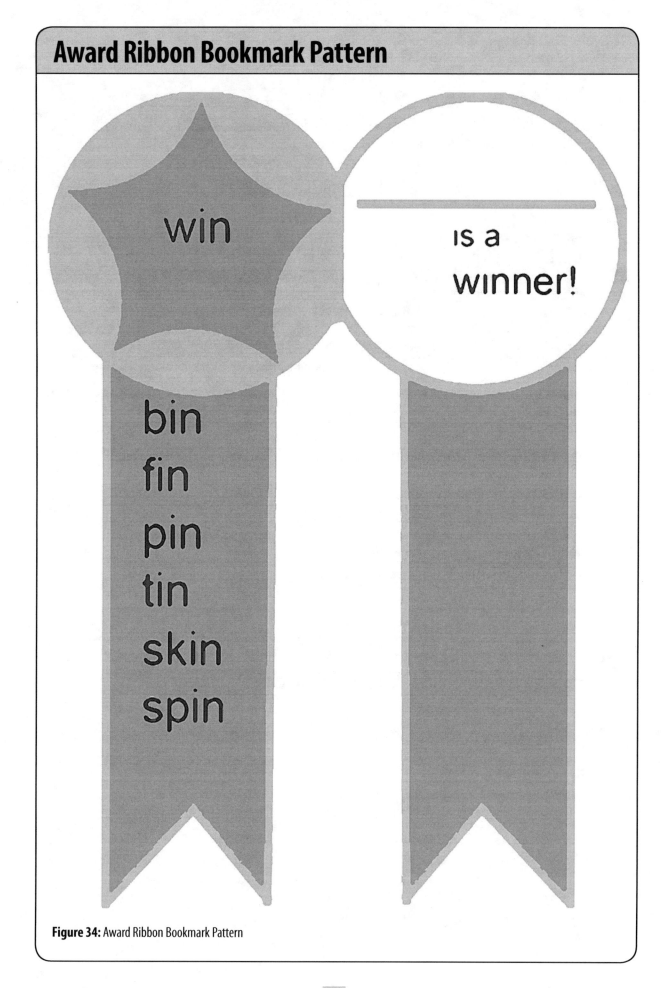

Figure 34: Award Ribbon Bookmark Pattern

Unit 16: The *-ink* Rime

PRESENTING THE VERSE

Here is a nonsense verse about a strange appearance at a local roller rink. Before you read the verse to the class, place cards for the *-ink* words in a pink box or bag. Target words include *blink, drink, link, pink, rink, sink, wink, shrink, stink,* and *think*. Introduce each one by saying, for example, "I am thinking of a word. It starts with *r* and it rhymes with *pink*. The word is _____." (rink) Pull out the card and show it to participants after they answer. Encourage them to say the word again before returning it to the container.

　　After reading it through the first time, ask participants whether the events in the story are possible or just make-believe. Encourage them to give reasons for their answers. You can also add additional visits to the rink with other rosy-clad animals before Ann finally gives up and skates off to meet her flesh and blood companions. For example, a pig, duck, and goat could each, in turn, shrink and disappear.

A Shrinking Horse at the Roller Rink: A Nonsense Verse

Ann went down to the roller rink. She met a horse all dressed in pink.

The horse began to wink and blink. Ann did not know what to think.

Then, it said, "Wink, wink, blink, blink. (Wink an eye, then blink both eyes.)

Get me water from the sink! (Make your voice higher and higher as if you are shrinking.)

Hurry back before I shrink!"

Ann got some water, but, by the time she came back,

The horse had (pause) poof! (pause) disappeared! (sound amazed)

The next day (stretch this phrase out).

Ann went down to the roller rink. She met a cow all dressed in pink.

The cow began to wink and blink. Ann looked around, and, what do you think?

(Pause. If desired, you can ask participants what they think she did.)

She skated away to meet her friends.

Little Stinker: A Color and Fold Project

This simple tent-fold craft offers students a chance to explore the sense of smell, as well as to review –*ink* rhymes. Drip flavor extracts, essential oils such as lavender, or highly-scented food juices such as garlic or onion juice onto cotton balls. Encourage students to rub the cotton balls inside their folded skunks to create a delightfully smelly new dimension for their "Little Stinkers."

Figure 35: Photo of the Finished Little Stinker

Materials
- sample Little Stinker
- Little Stinker pattern pages
- scissors
- markers or crayons
- optional: cotton balls scented with peppermint, almond, vanilla, lemon, or orange extract, eucalyptus or lavender essential oil, or with garlic juice (do not use perfume since some students are allergic to it), a bowl or tray for the scented cotton balls

Directions
1. Allow time for students to discuss personal experiences with skunks. Establish that these animals protect themselves with a powerful scent.
2. Show the sample Little Stinker.
3. Distribute the pattern pages.
4. Tell students to cut along the heavy lines and fold on the dotted lines.
5. Encourage students to draw green plants in the background on each side of the page.
6. *Optional:* While they are working, walk around and offer participants a chance to select a cotton ball and add scent to their skunk.
7. Encourage participants to read the –*ink* words printed around the Little Stinker to their parents at home.

Little Stinker Pattern

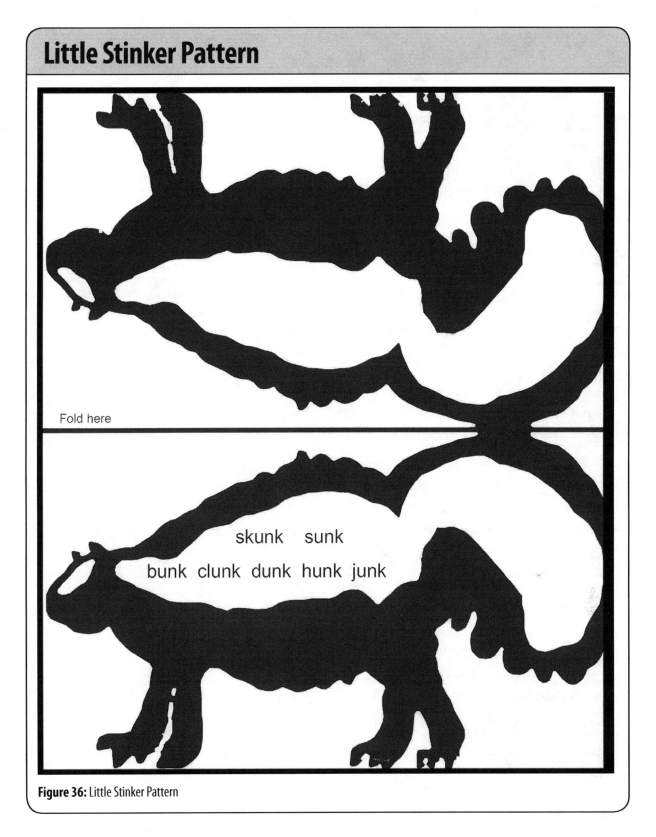

Fold here

skunk   sunk

bunk clunk dunk hunk junk

Figure 36: Little Stinker Pattern

SUGGESTED BOOKS TO COMPLETE THE PROGRAM

Pinkalicious by Victoria Kann

Mike Fink by Steven Kellogg

Magic Thinks Big by Elisha Cooper

I Stink! by Kate McMullan

Unit 17: The *–ock* Rime

PRESENTING THE VERSE

Use a chart, the board, or word cards to introduce the *–ock* rime words, which include *clock, stock, dock, lock, rock, sock, flock, knock, block, smock,* and *shock*. If desired, draw or paste a picture of a lock on the outside of a mailing envelope and place the word cards inside, or wear an artist's smock and pull the cards out of the pocket.

Encourage students to join in as you repeat each *–ock* rime in the verse "A Day at the Dock." Hold up the word card, or point to the word on the chart.

You can also encourage students to act out one or more of the "Knock Knock Mini-Plays" with partners.

A Day at the Dock: A Participation Verse

Mike was bored and watching the clock. Clock, clock, clock, clock.

All of a sudden, he heard a knock. Knock, knock, knock, knock.

His best friend Sam led him down the block. Block, block, block, block.

They walked through town and down to the dock. Dock, dock, dock, dock.

They spotted a seal asleep on a rock. Rock, rock, rock, rock.

Some gulls took off in a big white flock. Flock, flock, flock, flock.

An artist was painting. He wore a smock. Smock, smock, smock, smock.

Sam lost the key to his front door lock. Lock, lock, lock, lock.

They looked for it by the artist's smock, the seagull flock, the seal on the rock, the fishing dock, on Mike's own block, and under the clock.

Tick, tock, tick, tock. Sam's lost key was under the clock.

Knock Knock: Three Mini-Plays

Person 1: Knock knock

Person 2: Who's there?

Person 1: Tick

Person 2: Tick who?

Person 1: Tick Tock

Person 1: Knock knock

Person 2: Who's there?

Person 1: Alpha Bet

Person 2: Alpha Bet who?

Person 1: Alpha Bet Block

Person 1: Knock knock

Person 2: Who's there?

Person 1: Grandfather

Person 2: Grandfather who?

Person 1: Grandfather Clock

SUGGESTED BOOKS TO COMPLETE THE PROGRAM

My Grandmother's Clock by Geraldine McCaughrean

Cluck O'Clock by Kes Gray

My Dog Is as Smelly as Dirty Socks: And Other Funny Family Portraits by Hanoch Piven

Unit 18: The *–ot* Rime

PRESENTING THE VERSE

Use a chart, the board, or word cards to introduce the *–ot* rime words, which include *cot, hot, lot, not, pot, rot, trot,* and *spot*. If desired, draw or paste a picture of a pot on the outside of a mailing envelope and place the word cards inside.

Read the verse through, holding up a word card of the *–ot* rime in each stanza. Read it again, encouraging the children to join in on all or part of each refrain.

Spit, Spat, Spot: A Participation Verse

A little old man had a cat named Spot. *Refrain:* Spit, spat, spot.

He lived in a cabin and slept on a cot. *Refrain:* Cut, cat, cot.

The cabin sat in a beautiful spot. *Refrain:* Spit, spat, spot.

He made his dinner in an old iron pot. *Refrain:* Pit, pat, pot.

It was always good and usually hot. *Refrain:* Hit, hat, hot.

He always had plenty, but never a lot. *Refrain:* Lit, let, lot.

That little old man was wiser than not. *Refrain:* Nut, net, not.

Hot or Not: A Show-Your-Card Activity

Children are burned or injured by hot things every day. Review the *–ot* rime, emphasize some important safety rules, reinforce categorization skills, and teach the concept of warm and cool colors in art, all with this simple, self-evaluating activity.

Materials
- paper
- watercolor markers in dark colors

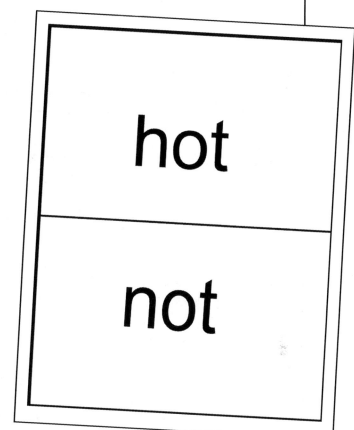

Figure 37: Finished Hot and Not Card

Directions

1. Help children print two word cards on plain paper. One will say hot. The other will say not. Have them draw a box around each word, and then color the rest of the hot card with a warm color (yellow, orange, or red) and the rest of the not card with a cool color (green, blue, or purple).

2. Read items from the list below, or show pictures of similar items. Children should hold up either the hot or not card for each item. If there is disagreement, stop the activity for a quick discussion.

3. After the activity, encourage students to draw something that is hot and something that is not.

4. Use student drawings on a bulletin board to illustrate safety rules relating to heat.

Things That Are Hot or Cold

ice	coffee	space
fire	lemonade	mountain
snow	refrigerator	lake
sun	stove	boiling water
burner		

SUGGESTED BOOKS TO COMPLETE THE PROGRAM

Hot Hippo by Mwenye Hadithi

A Lot of Otters by Barbara Helen Berger

How Chipmunk Got His Stripes by Joseph Bruchac

The Empty Pot by Demi

Unit 19: The *–og* Rime

PRESENTING THE VERSE

Use a chart, the board, or word cards to introduce the *–og* rime words, which include *bog, dog, hog, fog, jog, log,* and *frog*. If desired, draw or paste a picture of a dog and doghouse on the outside of a mailing envelope and place the word cards inside.

Read the "One Morning in the Fog" all the way through. Then, read it a second time, and encourage participants to join in on the second and third lines of each stanza.

After the reading, help students discuss sounds that they might hear in different places. For example, in the city, they might hear sirens, car horns, and the cooing of pigeons. Invite participants to be very quiet, close their eyes, and listen for sounds in the room.

One Morning in the Fog: A Participation Verse

One morning in the fog, in the fog, in the fog; in the early, early fog.

I walked down to the bog, to the bog, to the bog; to the reedy, reedy bog.

I heard a barking dog, heard a dog, heard a dog; heard the barking of a dog.

I heard a croaking frog, heard a frog, heard a frog; heard the croaking of a frog.

I heard a grunting hog, heard a hog, heard a hog; heard the grunting of a hog.

(Reprise: pause for participants to fill in the missing *–og* rime. Hold up a word card or point to the word on a chart.)

I heard a barking (dog). I heard a croaking (frog). I heard a grunting (hog). In the reedy, reedy (bog); in the early morning fog, in the fog, in the fog; in the early morning fog.

Frog: A Color, Cut, and Fold Project

This funny little frog will help your students share –og rimes with their families.

Materials
- sample frog
- frog patterns
- scissors
- markers or crayons
- staplers or tape

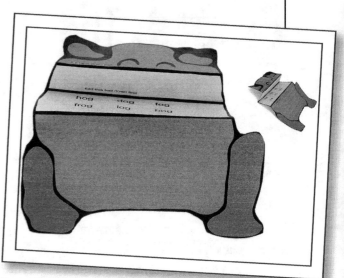

Figure 38: Photo of a Finished Frog

Directions
1. Share a picture book or poem about frogs.
2. Display the sample frog and demonstrate how it "talks."
3. Distribute the patterns and encourage children to color the eye and chin sections of the frog green. Tell them to color the inner, or mouth, sections pink.
4. Demonstrate how to cut out the frog.
5. Show students how to fold the frog on the line with the colored sections inside.
6. Demonstrate how to fold the eye and chin sections back, creating the mouth.
7. Help children cut out and staple or tape the finger strap to the outside of the upper mouth section. This will make the mouth easier to open and close.
8. Encourage students to make their puppets say all of the words in the frog's mouth. Challenge them to repeat the words to relatives at home.

SUGGESTED BOOKS TO COMPLETE THE PROGRAM

Frog and Toad Together by Arnold Lobel

A Frog in the Bog by Karma Wilson

Toad or Frog, Swamp or Bog? A Big Book of Nature's Confusables by Lynda Graham-Barber

A Huge Hog Is a Big Pig: A Rhyming Word Game by Francis McCall and Patricia Keeler

Frog Pattern

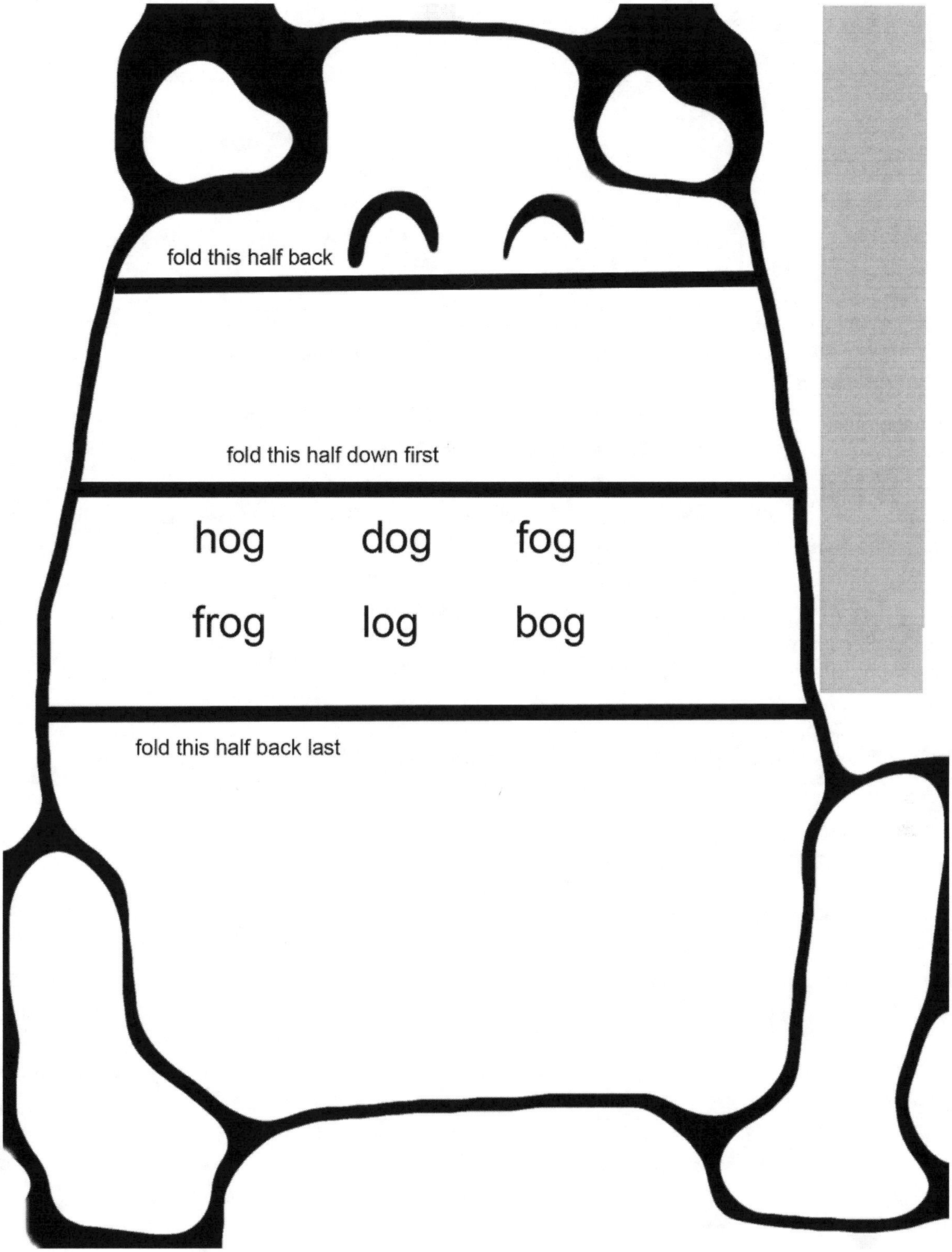

fold this half back
fold this half down first
hog dog fog
frog log bog
fold this half back last

Figure 39: Frog Pattern

Unit 20: The *–op* Rime

PRESENTING THE VERSE

Use a chart, the board, or word cards to introduce the *–op* rime words, which include *hop, mop, pop, top, crop, drop, flop,* and *clop.* If desired, draw or paste a picture of a top on the outside of a mailing envelope and place the word cards inside.

To introduce the verse, show a picture of a stagecoach. Talk about how people used to ride in such coaches before cars, trucks, buses, and airplanes were invented. Explain that, usually, people rode inside the coach and baggage was carried on top. Now, when people ride on stage coaches in amusement parks or while visiting Wild West resorts, they can ride on top if they prefer. Explain that they are about to take such a ride. Teach them the clip, clop, clip, clop refrain before beginning, and encourage them to join in.

Call five students to the front. Give one the *clop* card, another the *top* card, a third the *stop* card, a fourth the *drop* card, and the last the *hop* card. Tell them to hold up the card when they hear that word in the verse. Read slowly, and wait for their responses.

Stagecoach Ride: A Participation Verse

Here comes the stage! Clip, clop, clip, clop.

We'll ride on top. Clip, clop, clip, clop.

Some rain could fall. Drip, drop, drip, drop.

The horses will trot. Clip, clop, clip, clop.

At last they'll stop. Whoa, stop, whoa, stop!

And off we'll hop. Now, off we'll hop!

Go or Stop: An Action Activity

Review the –*op* rimes. Talk about pedestrian safety rules and street lights. Tell participants that they will be playing a stop and go game.

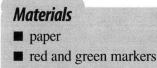

Materials
- paper
- red and green markers

Directions

1. Help children make two signs. One should be written in green and say *go*. The other should be written in red and say *stop*.
2. Initiate a simple action such as clapping in unison or chanting one of the –*op* rimes such as shop.
3. Invite each child, in turn, to start and stop the action by holding up either the *go* or the *stop* sign.
4. If you repeat the activity in a future session, encourage participants to think of other actions for the group to perform. If they can't think of any, here are some ideas to get them started.

Suggested Actions

chant an –*op* word	clap	shake head from side to side
tap head	tap knees	
shrug shoulders	tap heels	raise and lower arms
roll hands	nod head	

SUGGESTED BOOKS TO COMPLETE THE PROGRAM

Hop on Pop by Dr. Seuss

Flip Flop Bop by Matt Novak

Tops & Bottoms by Janet Stevens

Unit 21: The *—ug* Rime

PRESENTING THE VERSE

Use a chart, the board, or word cards to introduce the *—ug* rime words, which include *bug, dug, hug, mug, snug, rug,* and *tug.* If desired, draw or paste a picture of a bug on the outside of a mailing envelope and place the word cards inside.

Present the verse. After you read each refrain, pause to allow participants to repeat it. Point to the words on a chart, or hold up word cards.

The Hug Bug: A Participation Verse

Once there was a hugging bug. *Refrain:* Hug bug, hug bug.

Once there was a hugging bug. *Refrain:* That bug hugged all day.

In soft dirt the hug bug dug. *Refrain:* Bug dug, bug dug.

In soft dirt, the hug bug dug. *Refrain:* That bug dug all day.

Underground the bug was snug. *Refrain:* Snug bug, snug bug.

Underground the bug was snug. *Refrain:* The bug was snug all day.

My brother caught him in a mug. *Refrain:* Mug bug, mug bug.

My brother caught him in a mug, and there he stayed all day.

But then he crawled out on the rug. *Refrain:* Rug bug, rug bug.

But then he crawled out on the rug. *Refrain:* That's how he got away.

Hug Bug Arm Band: A Color, Cut, and Tape Project

Participants can wear their own hug bugs home on their arms and share the –*ug* words with friends and relatives.

Materials
- sample Hug Bug arm band
- Hug Bug arm band pattern
- scissors
- crayons or markers

Directions
1. Display the sample Hug Bug arm band.
2. Distribute Hug Bug patterns and invite participants to read the –*ug* words printed on them.
3. Encourage children to color their bugs.
4. Demonstrate how to cut out the bug.
5. Help students loop the bands around their upper arms or wrists and tape the ends together.

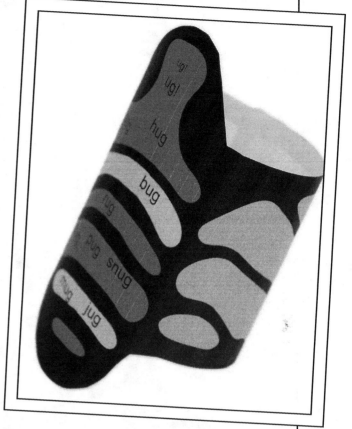

Figure 40: Photo of the Finished Hug Bug Arm Band

SUGGESTED BOOKS TO COMPLETE THE PROGRAM

Big Bug Surprise by Julia Gran

The Giant Hug by Sandra Horning

Bugs! Bugs! Bugs! by Bob Barner

Because a Little Bug Went Ka-Choo! by Rosetta Stone

Hug Bug Arm Band Pattern

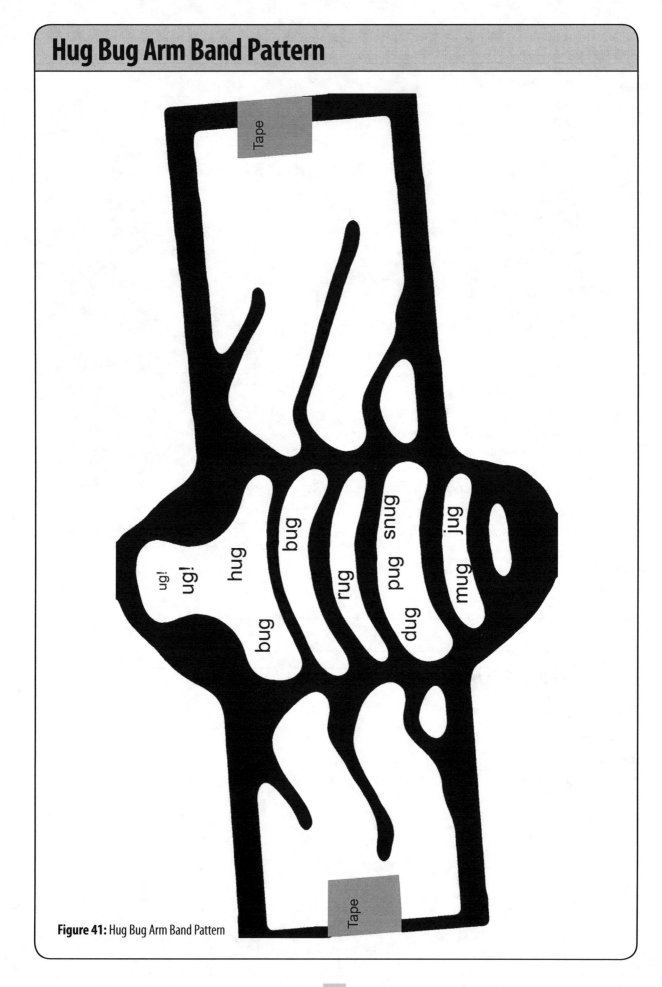

Figure 41: Hug Bug Arm Band Pattern

Unit 22: The –*uck* Rime

PRESENTING THE VERSE

Use a chart, the board, or word cards to introduce the –*uck* rime words, which include *buck, duck, luck, tuck, truck, muck, stuck,* and *cluck*. Warning: On this one, it might not be a good idea to ask children to volunteer their own words. If desired, draw or paste a picture of a truck on the outside of a mailing envelope and place the word cards inside.

Present the rhyme. Discuss whether Lucky really brought good luck, or whether he just happened to be there when something good happened. Invite students to share experiences with good or bad luck.

Lucky Ducky Day: A Participation Verse

Lucky was a lucky duck, lucky duck, lucky duck. Lucky was a lucky duck. Lucky, ducky day!

Once he saw a pickup truck, pickup truck, pickup truck.

Once he saw a pickup truck. Lucky, ducky day!

The truck was heading toward some muck, toward some muck, toward some muck.

The truck was heading toward some muck. Ucky, mucky day!

It hit some mud, then got stuck, then got stuck, then got stuck.

It hit some mud, then got stuck. Ucky, mucky day!

The barnyard hens began to cluck, began to cluck, began to cluck.

The barnyard hens began to cluck. Ucky, mucky day!

Then, over waddled Lucky Duck, Lucky Duck, Lucky Duck.

Then, over waddled Lucky Duck, Lucky, ducky day!

That truck began to rock and buck, rock and buck, rock and buck.

That truck began to rock and buck. And then it drove away.

Did Lucky really bring good luck, bring good luck, bring good luck?

Did Lucky really bring good luck? What does _____ say?

Lucky Duck: A Color, Cut, and Fold Project

Review the *–uck* rime with this cute little stand-up paper duck. For an easy display, make several ducks and place them on a blue paper or aluminum foil "pond."

Materials
- sample Lucky Duck
- Lucky Duck patterns
- scissors
- orange markers or crayons
- glue or tape

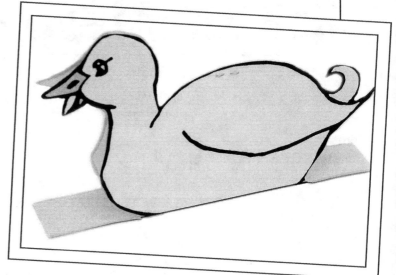

Figure 42: Photo of Finished Duck

Directions
1. Show students a sample Lucky Duck.
2. Distribute the patterns. Encourage participants to read the *–uck* words.
3. Invite children to color the duck's bill orange.
4. Demonstrate how to cut out the duck and fold it.
5. Help students glue or tape the flaps together so the duck can stand.
6. Encourage students to read the *–uck* words to friends and relatives at home.

SUGGESTED BOOKS TO COMPLETE THE PROGRAM

Duck for President by Doreen Cronin

Giggle, Giggle, Quack by Doreen Cronin

Good Luck, Mrs. K.! by Louise Borden

Chuck's Truck by Peggy Perry Anderson

Lucky Duck Pattern

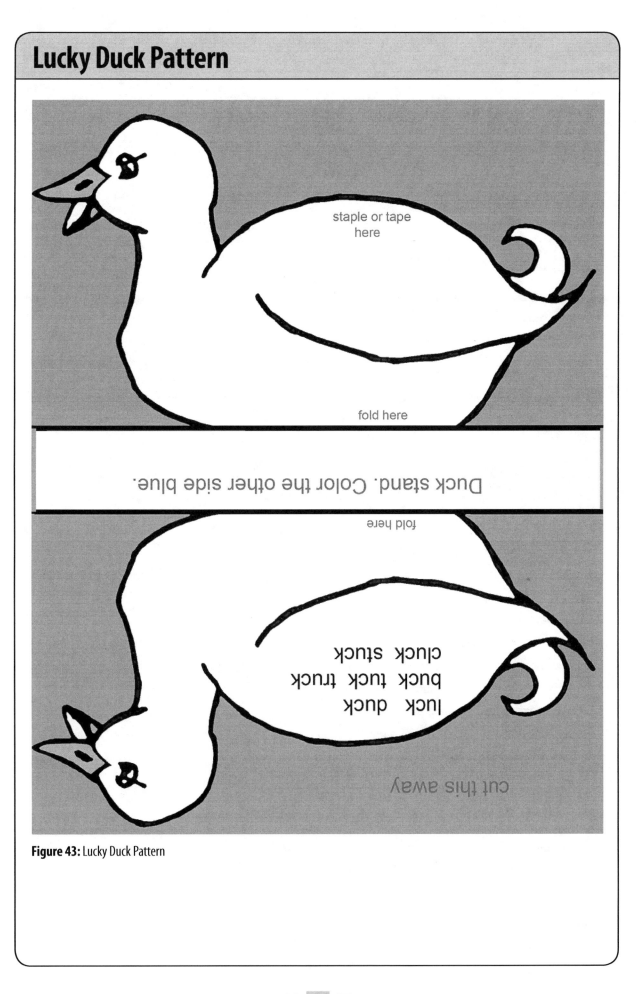

Figure 43: Lucky Duck Pattern

Unit 23: The *−ump* Rime

PRESENTING THE VERSE

Use a chart, the board, or word cards to introduce the *−ump* rime words, which include *bump, dump, hump, lump, pump, stump, clump,* and *jump.* If desired, draw or paste a picture of a stump on the outside of a mailing envelope and place the word cards inside.

Ask students if they have ever been to a baseball game. Explain that the park loudspeaker sometimes broadcasts a cheer. Say they will be using the rhythm of that cheer. Demonstrate "ump, ump, ump, ump" and have them repeat. Then, read the verse. Pause after each clue for participants to chant the appropriate *−ump* word, using the ballpark rhythm. Follow the directions at the end of the verse to review the words.

Ump! Ump! Ump! Ump! A Pattern Participation Verse

Leader: Ump! Ump! Ump! Ump! (Hint: Think of the build-up to a "charge!" at the ballpark.)

Participants: Ump! Ump! Ump! Ump!

Leader: When you cut a tree down, you are left with the stump! stump! stump! stump!

Participants: stump! stump! stump! stump!

Leader: On a camel's back, you'll see a hump! hump! hump! hump!

Participants: hump! hump! hump! hump!

Leader: When you throw away trash, it goes to the dump! dump! dump! dump!

Participants: dump! dump! dump! dump!

Leader: If you have a well, you need a pump! pump! pump! pump!

Participants: pump! pump! pump! pump!

Leader: To cross a creek, you have to jump! jump! jump! jump!

Participants: jump! jump! jump! jump!

Read the clues from the verse again. Pause after each and hold up a word card.

tree/stump	camel/hump	trash/dump
well/pump	creek/jump	

A Camel with a Hump: A Color and Fold Project

This stand-up favorite from the zoo will help students review the –*ump* rimes they used in the verse.

Materials

■ sample camel
■ camel patterns
■ scissors
■ markers or crayons

Figure 44: Photo of a Finished Camel

Directions

1. Show participants the sample camel.
2. Distribute the camel patterns. Encourage students to read the –*ump* rimes printed on the page.
3. Encourage children to color the camels and add a desert background to each side.
4. Show them how to fold the page along the line to create a free-standing picture.
5. Invite students to share the –*ump* words on the camel with friends and parents.

SUGGESTED BOOKS TO COMPLETE THE PROGRAM

Hop Jump by Ellen Stoll Walsh
Jump Rope Magic by Afi Scruggs
Bumpety Bump! by Pat Hutchins
A Truck Goes Rattley-Bumpa by Jonathan London

Camel Pattern

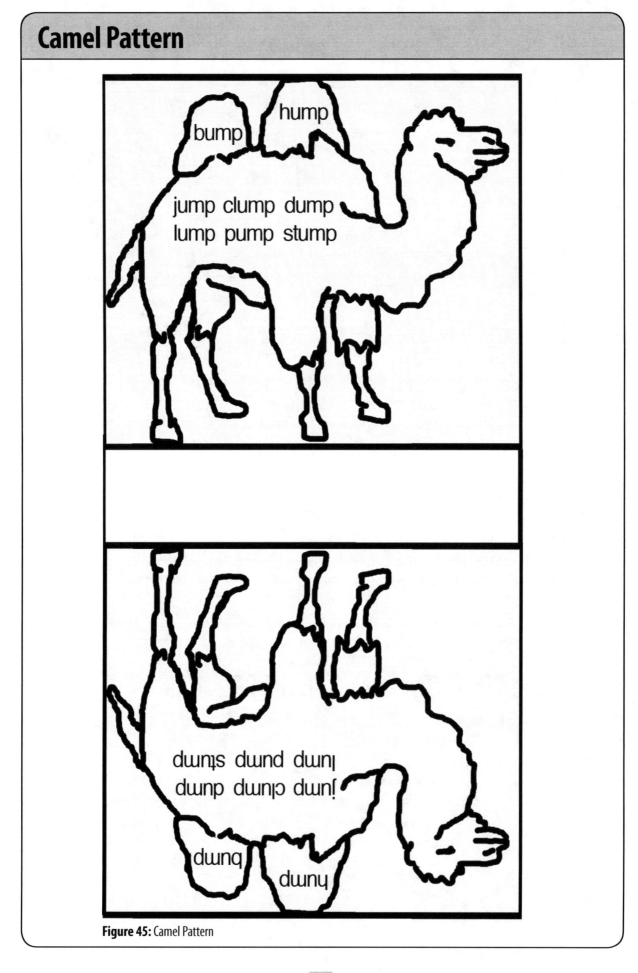

Figure 45: Camel Pattern

Unit 24: The *–unk* Rime

PRESENTING THE VERSE

Use a chart, the board, or word cards to introduce the *–unk* rime words, which include *bunk, dunk, hunk, sunk, trunk, clunk, shrunk,* and *junk.* If desired, draw or paste a picture of a steamer trunk on the outside of a mailing envelope and place the word cards inside.

Teach the repeating line "Plinkity Plankity Plunk" and a cue, such as pointing to them, to the group. Encourage participants to repeat the line as you present the rhyme about an old shed filled with forgotten treasures. Hold up a word card, or point to a chart when you say one of the *–unk* rimes.

Plinkity Plankity Plunk: A Participation Verse

Plinkity plankity plunk, this shed's filled with junk.

Plinkity plankity plunk, part of a ship that's sunk.

Plinkity plankity plunk, part of a sailor's bunk.

Plinkity plankity plunk, a flannel shirt that's shrunk.

Plinkity plankity plunk, some books from an old trunk.

Plinkity plankity plunk, something just went clunk!

Plinkity plankity plunk, I think I smell a skunk.

Forget the plankity plunk! Phew!

This Elephant Needs a Trunk: A Color and Cut Project

This funny little elephant face will help participants practice their –*unk* rimes.

Materials
- sample elephant face
- elephant face patterns
- scissors
- crayons or markers
- glue, glue sticks, staplers, or tape

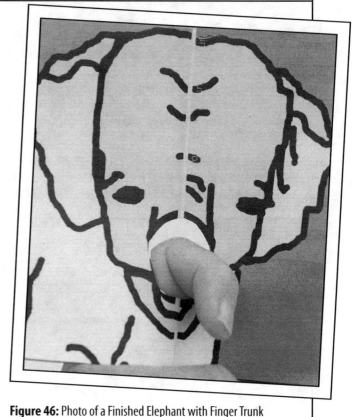

Figure 46: Photo of a Finished Elephant with Finger Trunk

Directions
1. Show students the sample elephant face.
2. Distribute the elephant face patterns.
   Encourage students to read the –*unk* words printed on the page.
3. Invite participants to color both elephant faces.
4. Demonstrate how to cut out the face shape and fold it over so there is a face on the front and one on the back.
5. Tell children to glue, tape, or staple the front and back sections together.
6. Demonstrate how to fold on the center vertical line to cut a hole for the finger "trunk."
7. Invite children to make the elephants move their trunks.

SUGGESTED BOOKS TO COMPLETE THE PROGRAM

Happy Dog Sizzles! by Lisa Grubb

Clink, Clank, Clunk by Miriam Aroner

Little Elephant's Trunk by Hazel Lincoln

Tanka Tanka Skunk! by Steve Webb

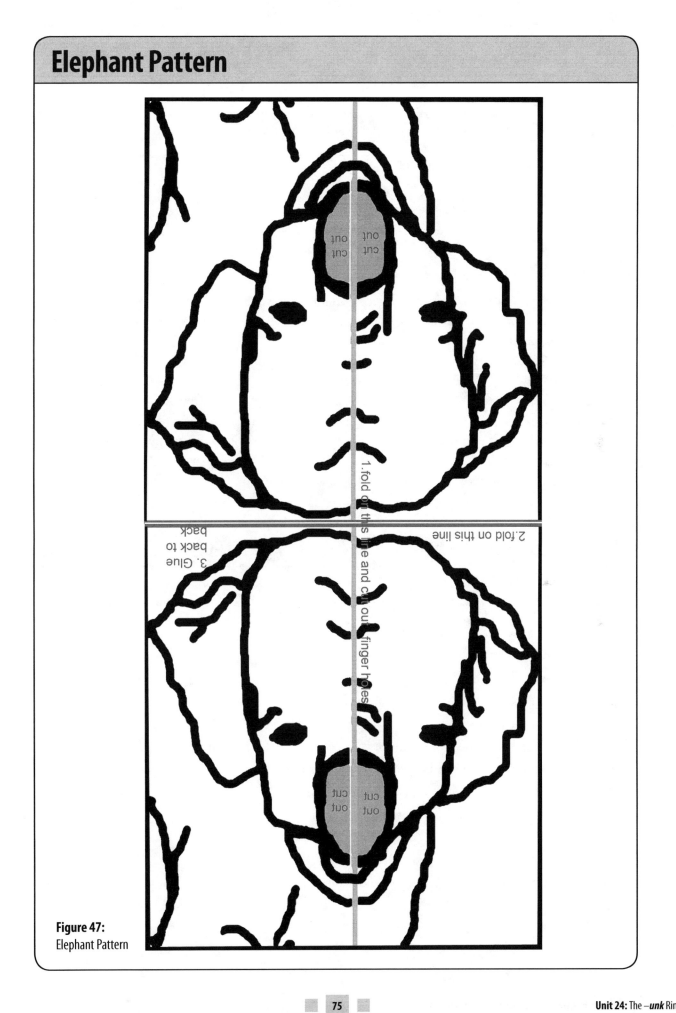

Figure 47:
Elephant Pattern

Unit 25: The *-ain* Rime

PRESENTING THE VERSE

Use a chart, the board, or word cards to introduce the *-ain* rime words, which include *gain, main, pain, rain, stain, train, drain, grain,* and *plain*. If desired, draw or paste a picture of a train on the outside of a mailing envelope and place the word cards inside.

Invite participants to talk about things they like to do in the rain. Tell them they will be taking a different kind of adventure in wet weather. Rehearse the first stanza with them. Encourage them to join you on each repeated line. Choose a child to show the *-ain* rime cards in order, or to point to them on a chart. If desired, put the whole verse on charts or on a transparency. Invite participants to read along with you. All of the words should be familiar, and there is a great deal of repetition. If there is time left after sharing the verse, consider showing students a few pictures of Spain from the library media collection, from a Web site if you have an e-media projector, or from a photo essay book.

What Can You Do in the Rain? A Participation Verse

What can you do in the rain? Oh, what can you do in the rain?

Can you ride on a train? Oh, can you ride on a train?

Yes, you can ride a train, oh, ride a train in the rain.

What can you do in the rain? Oh, what can you do in the rain?

Ride across the plain, oh, ride across the plain?

Yes, you can ride a train, oh, across the plain in the rain.

What can you do in the rain? Oh, what can you do in the rain? What can you do in the rain?

Can you see growing grain, oh, can you see growing grain?

Yes, you can ride a train, oh, ride it across the plain, oh,

To see some growing grain, oh, in the rain, oh, in the rain.

What can you do in the rain? What can you do in the rain?

Can you travel in Spain, oh, can you travel in Spain?

Yes, you can ride a train, oh, ride it across the plain, oh,

To see some growing grain, oh, away in beautiful Spain, oh, on a rainy plain in Spain!

A Plain Train: A Color and Fold Project

This little train will remind participants of the *–ain* words they learned in their trip across the rainy plain in Spain.

Materials
- sample train
- train patterns
- markers or crayons

Figure 48: Photo of a Finished Tent-Fold Train

Directions

1. Show students the sample train. Point out that it is part of a freight train. If desired, share a picture book about a freight train.
2. Distribute train patterns. Invite students to read the *–ain* words on the page.
3. Encourage participants to color the train and background above and below the fold line.
4. Demonstrate how to fold the train pattern so it will stand.
5. Encourage students to read the words to friends and relatives at home.

SUGGESTED BOOKS TO COMPLETE THE PROGRAM

Tuff Fluff: The Case of Duckie's Missing Brain by Scott Nash
Rain Player by David Wisniewski

Plain Train Pattern

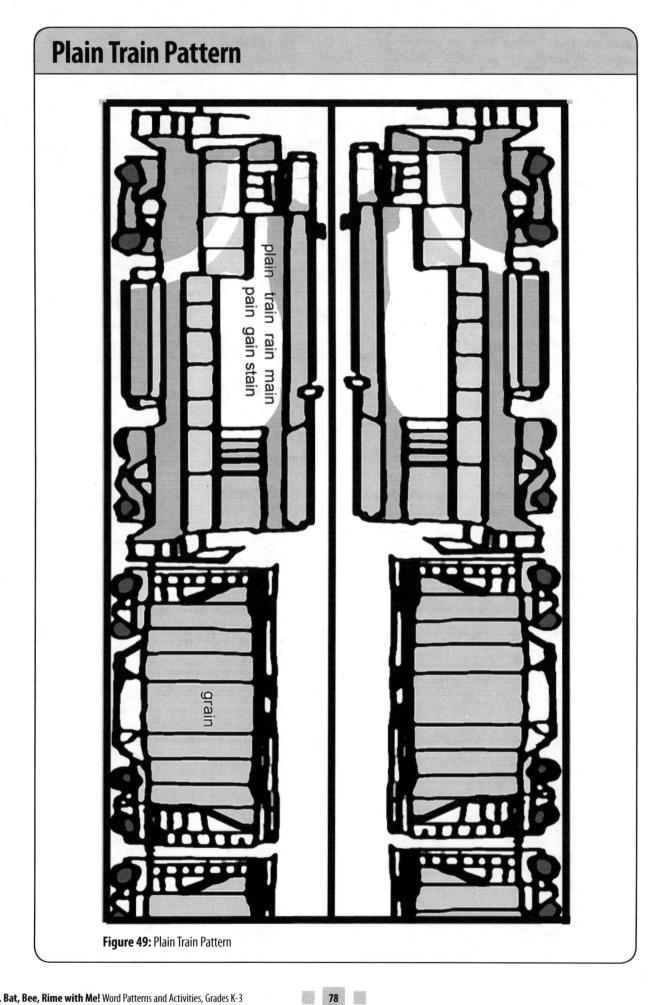

plain train rain main
pain gain stain

grain

Figure 49: Plain Train Pattern

Unit 26: The *–ake* Rime

PRESENTING THE VERSE

Use a chart, the board, or word cards to introduce the *–ake* rime words, which include *bake, cake, fake, lake, make, rake, take, wake,* and *stake*. If desired, draw or paste a picture of a cake on the outside of a mailing envelope and place the word cards inside.

Read the first stanza of "Today is Monday, Let's Bake a Cake" to establish the pattern. Divide up the group for the response lines. Instead of using boys and girls, you may choose to divide the room in half down the middle. When presenting later stanzas, pause after each line in the reprise to see if children can supply the activity for each day. Adding actions will make the verse more memorable.

Today Is Monday. Let's Bake a Cake: A Cumulative Action Verse

Today is Monday. Let's bake a cake. (Suggested action: hold an imaginary bowl in one arm and stir with the opposite hand.)
Boys: Let's bake a cake. *Girls:* Let's bake a cake. Today is Monday. Let's bake a cake.
Monday, bake a cake, hip, hip, hooray! (Suggested action: raise one or both hands in a cheer.)

Today is Tuesday. Let's sweep and rake. (Suggested action: pretend to hold a rake with both hands and pull it toward you.)
Boys: Let's sweep and rake. *Girls:* Let's sweep and rake. Today is Tuesday. Sweep and rake.
Tuesday, sweep and rake; Monday, bake a cake; hip, hip, hooray!

Today is Wednesday. Let's row at the lake. (Suggested action: pretend to row a boat.)
Boys: Let's row on the lake. *Girls:* Let's row on the lake. Today is Wednesday. Row on the lake.
Wednesday, row on the lake; Tuesday, sweep and rake; Monday, bake a cake; hip, hip, hooray!

Today is Thursday. Let's shimmy and shake. (Suggested action: wiggle around.)
Boys: Let's shimmy and shake. *Girls:* Let's shimmy and shake. Today is Thursday. Shimmy and shake.
Thursday, shimmy and shake; Wednesday, row on the lake; Tuesday, sweep and rake; Monday, bake a cake; hip, hip, hooray!

Today is Friday. Let's hold a snake. (Suggested action: pretend to hold up a wiggly snake with both hands.)

Boys: Let's hold a snake. *Girls:* Let's hold a snake. Today is Friday. Hold a snake.

Friday, hold a snake; Thursday, shimmy and shake; Wednesday, row on the lake; Tuesday, sweep and rake; Monday, bake a cake; hip, hip, hooray!

Today is Saturday. Let's feed a drake. (Suggested action: hold out a hand as if feeding a duck.)

Boys: Let's feed a drake. *Girls:* Let's feed a drake. Today is Saturday. Feed a drake.

Saturday, feed a drake; Friday, hold a snake; Thursday, shimmy and shake; Wednesday, row on the lake; Tuesday, sweep and rake; Monday, bake a cake; hip, hip, hooray!

Today is Sunday for goodness sake! (Suggested action: look pleased, shrug, and hold hands out from bent elbows as if to say, "don't we deserve a day off?")

Boys: for goodness sake! *Girls:* for goodness sake! Today is Sunday for goodness sake!

Saturday, feed a drake; Friday, hold a snake; Thursday, shimmy and shake; Wednesday, row on the lake; Tuesday, sweep and rake; Monday, bake a cake; hip, hip, hooray!

B –*ake*, Bake: A Dramatic Play Activity

This dramatic play activity will help students review the –*ake* rimes. It can be used for other rimes as well. The cards or sheets can be saved in a folder and used for several years. Lamination will make them last even longer.

Materials
- One word card or copy paper page with the letters –*ake* for each pair of participants. The letters should be large enough to be seen by all students in the group.
- One initial consonant or blend for each pair of participants. These do not really have to be cards. Each sheet can be a large letter printed on half a sheet of copy paper. The letters should be the same size as those on the –*ake* pages. Put only one letter on each card or half-page. Use one each of the following letters: b, c, dr, f, l, m, r, s, t, w. If your group is larger, make an additional set. Cut the pages before distributing them to students. Each pair of participants should get an initial consonant and an –*ake* sheet or card.

Directions
1. Encourage each participant to select a partner.
2. Distribute one –*ake* card and an initial consonant to each pair of students. (Each set of partners will be making a different word.)
3. Choose one pair of partners to use as an example. Tell the partner holding the –*ake* card to pretend he is waiting for someone. He should hold the card so everyone can see it. Take the other partner aside and whisper that he should run, hop, skip, or gallop in to meet his friend, then hold one of the letter cards in front of the –*ake* to make a word. Help him decide on his action before he does it. When the word is assembled in front of the group, the demonstration partners should wait. Whisper to them that they should say, "What does it say?" The group should respond, then each partner should read his part of the word. For example, l (l sound) –*ake*. Then, together, they should say "lake."
4. Allow the other partners time to decide on their movements and rehearse their words. Walk around and provide assistance.
5. Select volunteers to present their words to the group.

SUGGESTED BOOKS TO COMPLETE THE PROGRAM

The Great Cake Bake by Helen Ketteman

Make Way for Ducklings by Robert McCloskey

Don't Wake Up the Bear! by Marjorie Dennis Murray

Unit 27: The *—ail* Rime

PRESENTING THE VERSE

Use a chart, the board, or word cards to introduce the *—ail* rime words, which include *bail, fail, hail, mail, nail, pail, rail, sail, tail, trail,* and *snail*. If desired, draw or paste a picture of a snail on the outside of a mailing envelope and place the word cards inside.

Explain to participants that this verse is a memory challenge and that you are sometimes forgetful, so you might need their help. After you read the first line, invite students to coach you on the second line. Then, add the concluding phrase. Repeat this pattern. After completing the verse, repeat it, encouraging students to help you all the way through. Share word cards as hints.

Snail Trail: A Cumulative Verse

This morning a snail left a silvery trail. It went around a yellow pail.

This morning a snail left a silvery trail. It went around a yellow pail.

It went around a sailboat sail.

This morning a snail left a silvery trail. It went around a yellow pail.

It went around a sailboat sail. It went around my blue kite's tail.

This morning a snail left a silvery trail. It went around a yellow pail.

It went around a sailboat sail. It went around my blue kite's tail.

It went around some old junk mail.

This morning a snail left a silvery trail. It went around a yellow pail.

It went around a sailboat sail. It went around my blue kite's tail. It went around some old junk mail.

It went around a rusty nail.

This morning a snail left a silvery trail. It went around a yellow pail. It went around a sailboat sail.

It went around my blue kite's tail. It went around some old junk mail. It went around a rusty nail. It went across an iron hand rail.

This morning a snail left a silvery trail.

Snail: A Color and Fold Project

This little snail will help participants remember –*ail* sounds.

Materials
- sample snail
- snail pattern
- crayons or markers
- scissors,
- staplers, tape, or glue

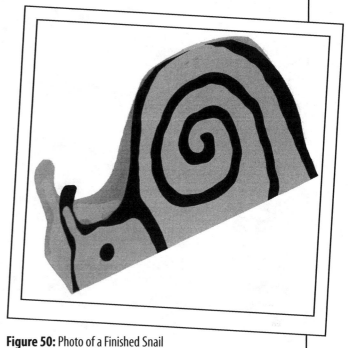

Figure 50: Photo of a Finished Snail

Directions
1. Discuss children's experience with snails. If you have not done so, read a picture book about snails such as *Are You a Snail?* by Judy Allen.
2. Display the sample snail.
3. Distribute the snail patterns.
4. Encourage participants to read the –*ail* rimes on the pattern.
5. Invite students to color both parts of the snail pattern.
6. Demonstrate how to cut out the snail and fold it.
7. Help children fasten the snail at the top with a staple, with tape, or with glue.
8. Encourage participants to read the words on the snail to friends and relatives at home.

SUGGESTED BOOKS TO COMPLETE THE PROGRAM

Are You a Snail? by Judy Allen

What Do You Do with a Tail Like This? by Robin Page

Mama Went to Jail for the Vote by Kathleen Karr

The Puddle Pail by Elisa Kleven

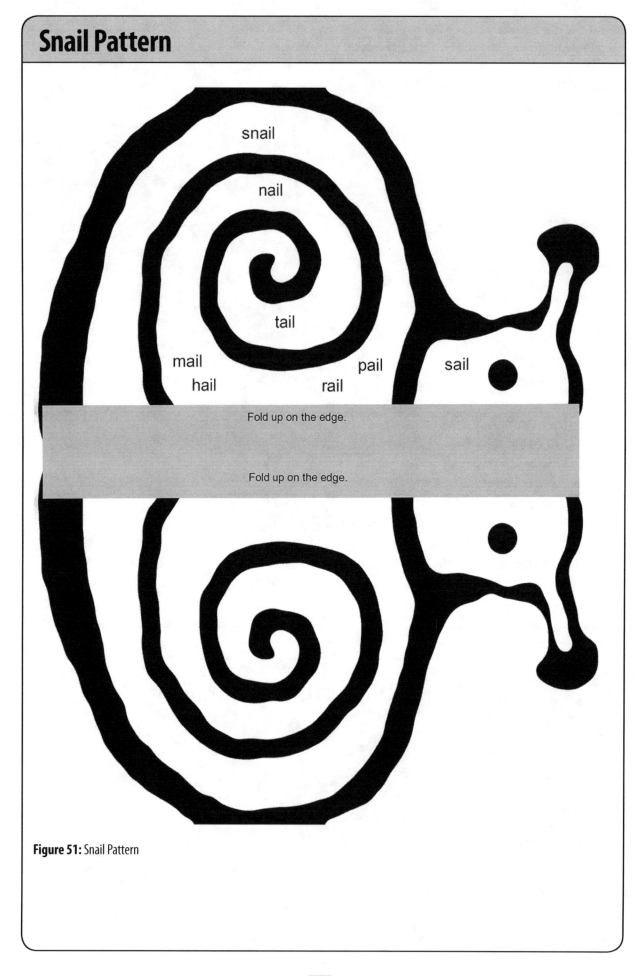

snail

nail

tail

mail

pail

sail

hail

rail

Fold up on the edge.

Fold up on the edge.

Figure 51: Snail Pattern

Unit 28: The *-ame* Rime

PRESENTING THE VERSE

Use a chart, the board, or word cards to introduce the *-ame* rime words, which include *blame, came, dame, fame, frame, game, lame, name, same,* and *tame.*

Explain that this verse is a ballad, a kind of poem that was popular in the days of castles, knights, and ladies. It repeats phrases and tells a story. Read it through, pausing, and inviting participants to say the *-ame* words. Hold up the word cards or point to the words. Read the rhyme again and encourage children to join in.

The Challenge of Boolameer: A Participation Verse

In the land of Boolameer, there lived wealthy dame.

A dame, a dame, there lived a wealthy dame.

In the spring of every year, she held a famous game.

A game, a game; she held a famous game.

From all over Boolameer brave knights and warriors came.

They came, they came; brave knights and warriors came.

Some of them were seeking love, others, might or fame.

Might or fame, might or fame; they wanted might or fame.

The prize she offered challengers was her fortune and her name.

Her name, her name; her fortune and her name.

Some of them came away scratched; others came away lame.

Came away lame, came away lame; they came away scratched or lame.

No matter how they came away, none was ever the same.

The same, the same; none was ever the same.

No matter how they came away, they had themselves to blame.

To blame, to blame; they had themselves to blame.

When they entered her great hall to play the risky game.

The game, the game; to play the risky game.

They came face to face with a picture in a frame.

A frame, a frame; a picture in a frame.

A lion stepped out of the picture. At first, he was very tame.

Very tame, very tame; the lion was very tame.

The challenger had three tries to guess that lion's name.

His name, his name; guess the lion's name.

Some thought it was Leo, others thought the same.

The same, the same; others thought the same.

Some tried King and Majesty, but none of them won the game.

The game, the game; none of them won the game.

At last, from far away, a brave contestant came.

He came, he came; a brave contestant came.

He faced the mighty lion and called out his own name.

His name, his name; he called out his own name.

From that day on, the winner lived in the home of the dame.

The dame, the dame; he lived in the home of the dame.

Both of them were happy and the lion stayed in his frame.

His frame, his frame; the lion stayed in his frame.

The Name Game: An Activity

Help students to hear initial sounds and to become more familiar with letter sounds in names with this game.

Materials
■ a shuffled set of word cards with a letter of the alphabet written on each one

Directions
1. Go around the circle and have each participant say his first name. After he says it, ask the group for that name's beginning letter.
2. Ask students for other names they have heard; for example, the names of sisters, brothers, uncles, aunts, or friends.
3. Take the deck of alphabet cards to the first student in the circle. Invite him to draw one, and then say a name that begins with that letter. If he can think of one, he may take the alphabet deck to any other player in the circle.
4. If a player cannot think of a name, he can call on a volunteer to offer one. Then, the volunteer may take the alphabet deck to the next player.
5. If nobody can think of a name, the player holding the deck may allow a player of his choosing to draw another letter.

Note: Silly names are fine, as long as they begin with the correct sound.

SUGGESTED BOOKS TO COMPLETE THE PROGRAM

The Name Quilt by Phyllis Root

My Name Is Yoon by Helen Recorvits

At the Same Time by Tom Tirabosco

Tacky and the Winter Games by Helen Lester

Unit 29: The *–ate* Rime

PRESENTING THE VERSE

Use a chart, the board, or word cards to introduce the *–ate* rime words, which include *ate, date, fate, gate, hate, late, mate, rate, crate, grate, plate, slate,* and *state*. If desired, draw or paste a picture of a gate on the outside of a mailing envelope and place the word cards inside.

     Read the first two lines of the verse. Ask participants what they notice. They should mention the repetition. Say they are very smart, and that you are betting that they will be able to help you with the next two lines. Continue this technique all the way through. Repeat the entire rhyme, displaying cards for the *–ate* words. If desired, pass out the cards, and invite students to hold up the appropriate one as the group says the word.

Michael, Close the Garden Gate: A Participation Verse

Michael, close the garden gate, garden gate, garden gate.

Michael, close the garden gate. Everyone is waiting.

The duck is out, and so's her mate, so's her mate, so's her mate.

The duck is out and so's her mate. All the geese are worried.

The dog is in an awful state, awful state, awful state.

The dog is in an awful state. He will not stop howling.

I know this is a chore you hate, chore you hate, chore you hate.

I know this is a chore you hate, but everyone is waiting.

Michael, close the garden gate, garden gate, garden gate.

Michael, close the garden gate. Everyone is waiting.

The Garden Gate: A Cut, Color, and Paste Project

This simple cut and color project creates a gate that opens and closes while reviewing *–ate* rimes from the verse.

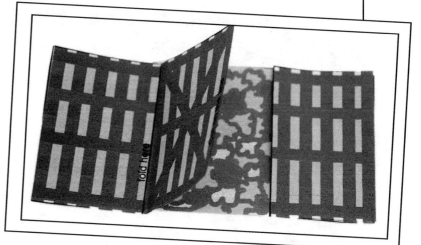

Figure 52: Finished Garden Gate

Materials
- sample garden gate
- gate patterns, markers
- glue sticks
- scissors

Directions
1. Display the sample garden gate.
2. Distribute the patterns.
3. Encourage students to read the *–ate* words.
4. Tell children to color the white square and the spaces between the fence pickets with flowers or bright colors.
5. Demonstrate how to cut out the fence section and fold the gate.
6. Help participants glue the fence section in place.
7. Encourage students to read the *–ate* rimes to friends and relatives at home.

SUGGESTED BOOKS TO COMPLETE THE PROGRAM

Don't Let the Pigeon Stay Up Late! by Mo Willems

Henry's Important Date by Robert M. Quackenbush

Now Everybody Really Hates Me by Jane Read Martin

Maybe a Bear Ate It! by Robie Harris

Garden Gate Pattern

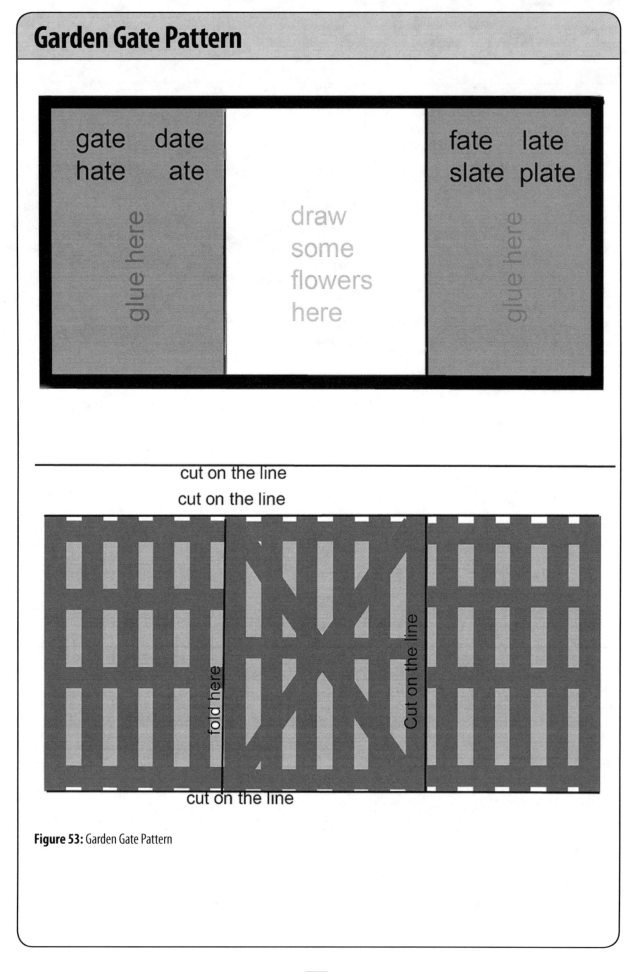

gate   date
hate   ate

glue here

draw
some
flowers
here

fate   late
slate   plate

glue here

cut on the line
cut on the line

fold here

Cut on the line

cut on the line

Figure 53: Garden Gate Pattern

Unit 30: The *−ay* Rime

PRESENTING THE VERSE

Use a chart, the board, or word cards to introduce the *−ay* rime words, which include *bay, day, hay, gray, lay, may, pay, ray, say, tray, way, stay,* and *play*. If desired, draw or paste a picture of a bale of hay on the outside of a mailing envelope and place the word cards inside.

Before reading "A Day in the Country," discuss places the children have visited. The poem travels to the country, the city, and the realm of the imagination. Take a minute to rehearse the refrain before starting each section of the verse. Choose a student or two to hold up word cards for the *−ay* rimes, or to point to the words on the chart.

The definition plays, with modification, can be used to review any rime. Reproduce the page, divide the group into partners, and allow children time to practice reading the parts. Invite a volunteer pair to present one of the definition plays to the group.

A Day in the Country: A Participation Verse

We went to the country one day, one day. We went to the country one day.

We climbed on a wagon and sat on some hay, when we went to the country one day.

We went to the country one day, one day. We went to the country one day.

We ran to the stream to splash and play, when we went to the country one day.

We went to the city one day, one day. We went to the city one day.

We went out to lunch and ate from a tray. We went to the city one day.

We went to the city one day, one day. We went to the city one day.

The buildings were tall and the sky was gray. We went to the city one day.

We went to the city one day, one day, when we went to the city one day.

We walked to the zoo and knew the way, when we went to the city one day.

We read a book one day, one day. We read a book one day.

We found a jewel with a magic ray. We read a book one day.

Night and Day: A Color and Fold Project

Just as the verse pointed out the differences between the city and country, this folded picture points out the differences between two other opposites—day and night.

Materials
- sample folded day and night picture, day and night patterns
- markers or crayons

Figure 54: Photo of the Finished Night and Day Folded Picture

Directions
1. Show the sample folded day and night picture.
2. Distribute the patterns and encourage students to read the *–ay* rimes printed on them.
3. Demonstrate how to color each part of the picture to reflect the correct time of day.
4. After children have finished coloring, show them how to fold the picture along the line so it will stand.
5. Encourage participants to share the *–ay* rimes printed on the picture with friends and relatives at home.

Night and Day Pattern

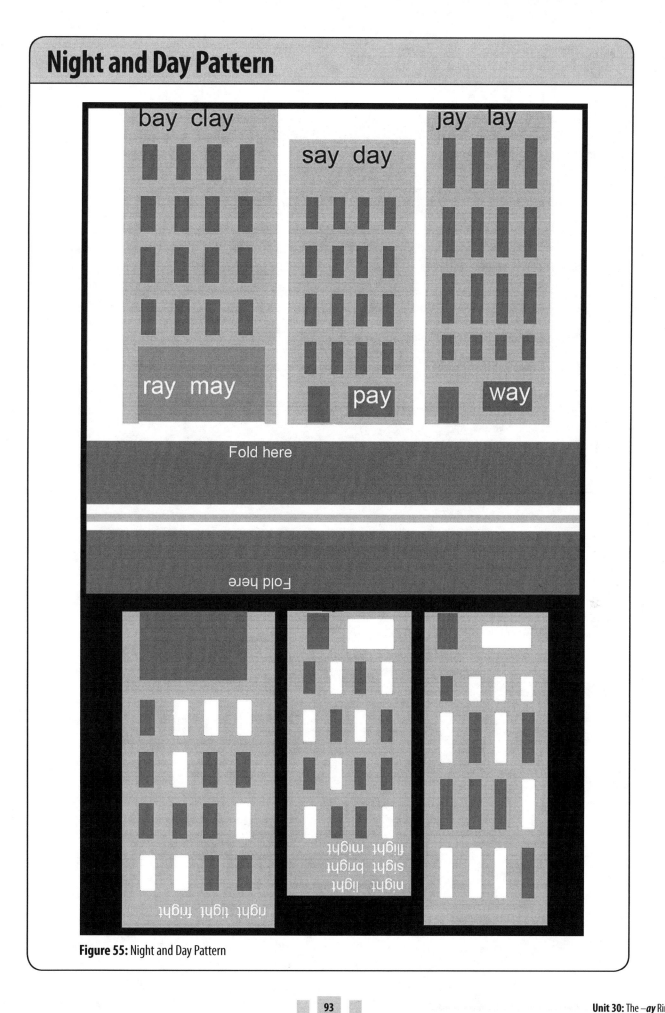

Figure 55: Night and Day Pattern

What Am I? Four Definition Plays

Player 1: I am made of light. My name rhymes with day. What am I?

Player 2: Are you a piece of clay?

Player 1: No, clay is not made of light.

Player 2: Of course not. You are made of light and rhyme with day. You are a ray!

Player 1: You guessed it. Hooray!

Player 1: I am lighter than black. My name rhymes with May. What am I?

Player 2: Blue is lighter than black. I like blue best of all.

Player 1: I like blue, too, but I am not blue. My name rhymes with May.

Player 2: I knew it all the time. You are gray.

Player 1: You guessed it. Hooray!

Player 1: I am a safe place for boats. My name rhymes with way. What am I?

Player 2: Are you a tray?

Player 1: That's silly. A tray is not a safe place for boats.

Player 2: I was just joking. I know who you are. You are a bay.

Player 1: You guessed it. Hooray!

Player 1: I am a month. My name rhymes with say. What am I?

Player 2: Are you hay?

Player 1: Stop kidding around! Hay is not a month.

Player 2: I know that. I just wanted to see what you would say. You are May.

Player 1: You guessed it. Hooray!

SUGGESTED BOOKS TO COMPLETE THE PROGRAM

Play Ball, Amelia Bedelia by Peggy Parish

Down by the Bay by Raffi

Look Both Ways: A Cautionary Tale by Diane Z. Shore

Unit 31: The —*eat* Rime

PRESENTING THE VERSE

Use a chart, the board, or word cards to introduce the —*eat* rime words, which include *eat, beat, heat, meat, neat, seat, treat,* and *wheat*.

When introducing the verse, encourage participants to talk about a person in their family who is always late to the dinner table. Invite them to imagine older brothers or sisters who are always busy combing their hair or looking in the mirror. Choose one or two volunteers to hold up cards for the repeated rimes in each stanza. Tell them to encourage everyone to join in.

Come, Sit Down and Eat: A Verse with a Beat, Beat, Beat

Neat, neat, neat, you are neat, neat, neat.

You are very clean, and, I repeat, you are clean and neat.

Seat, seat, seat, take your seat, seat, seat.

Everyone is ready. You are clean and neat.

And, I repeat, it's time to take a seat.

Treat, treat, treat, here's a treat, treat, treat.

Your favorite food is steaming. You are clean and neat.

It's time to take a seat, because, I repeat, we have your favorite treat.

Eat, eat, eat, now let's eat, eat, eat. The table's set and ready.

You are clean and neat. It's time to take a seat for your favorite treat.

And so, I repeat, come, sit down and eat.

Repeat, repeat, repeat, I repeat, repeat, repeat,

Everyone is ready. You are clean and neat. It's time to take a seat for your favorite treat.

Come, sit down and eat.

Once again, I repeat, come, sit down and eat.

Beat the Heat: A Mini-Play for Puppets or Pairs

Player 1: (waving a fan) I hate this heat.

Player 2: I know a way to beat it.

Player 1: You do? How?

Player 2: We could make a seat out of a great big ice cube. We could take turns sitting in it.

Player 1: That sounds good. Where will we get the ice cube?

Player 2: From a place where they keep meat. Those places are very cold.

Player 1: I do not think that would work.

Player 2: Why not?

Player 1: Where would we find a place that keeps meat?

Player 2: Okay, do you have a better idea?

Player 1: Yes, I do. We can go into the kitchen. Mom has some treats in the freezer.
(He leaves.)

Player 2: I still think an ice seat would be more fun.

Player 1: (he calls from off stage): I am eating a cherry treat. I am cooler already.

Player 2: (hurries off stage) Save a grape one for me!

SUGGESTED BOOKS TO COMPLETE THE PROGRAM

How Do Dinosaurs Eat Their Food? by Jane Yolen
I'd Really Like to Eat a Child by Sylviane Donnio
Froggy Eats Out by Jonathan London
This Is the Way We Eat Our Lunch: A Book about Children Around the World by Edith Baer

Unit 32: The *–ice* Rime

PRESENTING THE VERSE

Use a chart, the board, or word cards to introduce the *–ice* rime words, which include *dice, mice, nice, price, rice, slice,* and *twice*. If desired, draw or paste a picture of two mice on the outside of a mailing envelope and place the word cards inside.

Explain to participants that you are going to need help with this verse. Read the first line, and then pause. Say, "Where are you? I said I was going to need your help." Ask for the boys, the girls, the left side, and then the right side. When they are fully engaged in the activity, continue. Repeat the entire rhyme, holding up the word cards.

Anna Tice and Her Mice: A Say-It-Twice Verse

Anna Tice bought two mice. Now join in, and say it twice.

Anna Tice bought two mice. Anna Tice bought two mice.

Anna's mice were worth their price. Now join in and say it twice.

Anna's mice were worth their price. Anna's mice were worth their price.

Anna's mice were very nice. Now join in and say it twice.

Anna's mice were very nice. Anna's mice were very nice.

Anna's mice ate seeds and rice. Now join in and say it twice.

Anna's mice ate seeds and rice. Anna's mice ate seeds and rice.

Anna Tice loved those mice. Now join in and say it twice.

Anna Tice loved those mice. Anna Tice loved those mice.

Anna Tice bought two mice. (Participants repeat each line.)

Anna's mice were worth their price. Anna's mice were very nice. Anna's mice ate seeds and rice.

Anna Tice loved those mice!

Nice Mice: A Color and Fold Project

This simple color and fold activity will help participants remember the rimes introduced in the verse.

Materials
- sample mice
- patterns
- markers or crayons

Figure 56: Finished Nice Mice Project

Directions
1. Show participants the sample mice.
2. Distribute the pattern pages. Encourage students to read the words printed on the sheet.
3. Invite children to color the mice and to create a background. It could be an exercise wheel, a cage, or any other setting that seems appropriate.
4. Demonstrate how to fold the page so it will stand.
5. Encourage participants to share the words they have learned with friends and relatives at home.

SUGGESTED BOOKS TO COMPLETE THE PROGRAM

Mrs. Brice's Mice by Syd Hoff

Chicken Soup with Rice: A Book of Months by Maurice Sendak

Mama Provi and the Pot of Rice by Sylvia Rosa-Casanova

Each Orange Had 8 Slices by Paul Giganti

Nice Mice Pattern

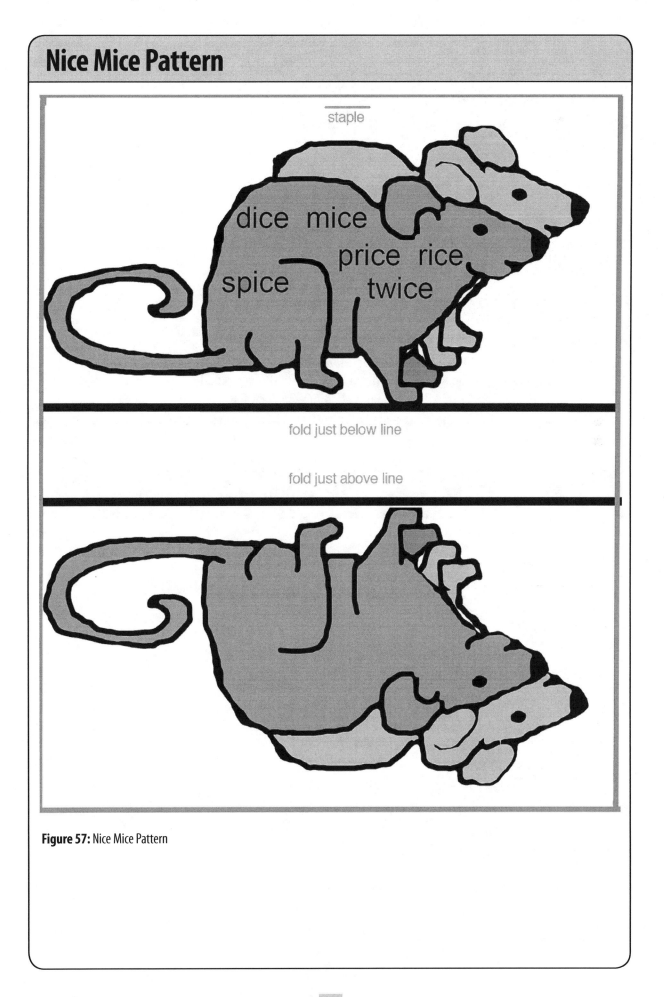

staple

dice mice

price rice

spice twice

fold just below line

fold just above line

Figure 57: Nice Mice Pattern

Unit 33: The *–ide* Rime

PRESENTING THE VERSE

Use a chart, the board, or word cards to introduce the *–ide* rime words, which include *hide, ride, side, tide, wide, bride, glide, slide,* and *pride*. If desired, paste a picture of a playground slide on the outside of a mailing envelope and place the word cards inside.

Teach students the refrain, "Silent and still sat Martin Zide." When participants are ready, read the first line, and then cue them. Go all the way through the verse. If there is additional time, give each word card to a small group of students. All participants should be included. Repeat the reading. This time, each small group should stand when the verse reaches their word. They should say their word, repeat the refrain, and then be seated.

Silent and Still Sat Martin Zide: A Participation Verse

The beach was long; the beach was wide.

Silent and still sat Martin Zide.

He saw runners run and surfers glide.

Silent and still sat Martin Zide.

He watched some kids on a playground slide.

Silent and still sat Martin Zide.

He saw fish leap and seagulls glide.

Silent and still sat Martin Zide.

He watched birds swoop and sand crabs hide.

Silent and still sat Martin Zide.

He saw a groom. He saw a bride.

Silent and still sat Martin Zide.

Then higher and higher rose the tide,

and back to his car strode Martin Zide.

A Ride: A Color, Cut, and Fold Project

Invite children to talk about car rides they remember before doing this color and fold activity.

Materials

- sample car
- pattern pages
- crayons or markers

Figure 58: Photo of the Finished Car

Directions

1. Display the sample car.
2. Distribute the pattern pages. Encourage students to read the words printed on the car.
3. Invite participants to color the car and add a background suggested by a remembered car trip.
4. Demonstrate how to fold the pattern so it will stand.
5. Encourage children to share the words printed on the car with friends and relatives at home.

SUGGESTED BOOKS TO COMPLETE THE PROGRAM

Tippy-Tippy-Tippy, Hide! by Candace Fleming

Ride a Purple Pelican by Jack Prelutsky

Slide Already! by Kit Allen

What's in the Tide Pool? by Anne Hunter

Car Pattern

Figure 59: Car Pattern

Unit 34: The *–ight* Rime

PRESENTING THE VERSE

Use a chart, the board, or word cards to introduce the *–ight* rime words, which include *delight, flight, fight, light, might, night, right, tight,* and *sight*. Ask students to tell about trips they have taken in planes. As you present the verse, point to every *–ight* word. Invite students to join you in saying the second line of each stanza.

Morgan Wright's Flight: A Participation Verse

Morgan Wright might take a flight, take a flight, take a flight.

Morgan Wright might take a flight all the way to China.

She might pull the seatbelt tight, seatbelt tight, seatbelt tight.

She might pull the seatbelt tight on her way to China.

Morgan Wright might fly at night, fly at night, fly at night.

Morgan Wright might fly at night on her way to China.

Morgan Wright might see dawn's light, see dawn's light, see dawn's light.

Morgan Wright might see dawn's light, on her way to China.

That might be a pretty sight, pretty sight, pretty sight.

That might be a pretty sight, on her way to China.

The sight might fill her with delight, with delight, with delight.

The sight might fill her with delight on her way to China.

Light Flight: A High-Flying Project

If you add a small paper clip to the nose of this little plane, it really soars!

Materials
- sample plane
- pattern pages
- scissors, markers
- small paper clips

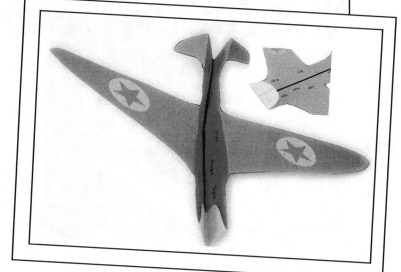

Figure 60: Photo of the Finished Plane

Directions
1. Show the sample plane.
2. Distribute the pattern pages and encourage students to read the words printed on the plane.
3. Encourage students to color the plane.
4. Demonstrate how to cut and fold the plane.
5. Invite students to share the words printed on the plane with friends and relatives at home.

SUGGESTED BOOKS TO COMPLETE THE PROGRAM

Flight of the Dodo by Peter Brown

The Glorious Flight: Across the Channel with Louis Bleriot July 25, 1909 by Alice Provensen

The Magic School Bus Taking Flight: A Book about Flight by Joanna Cole

Clorinda Takes Flight by Robert Kinerk

Paper Airline Pattern

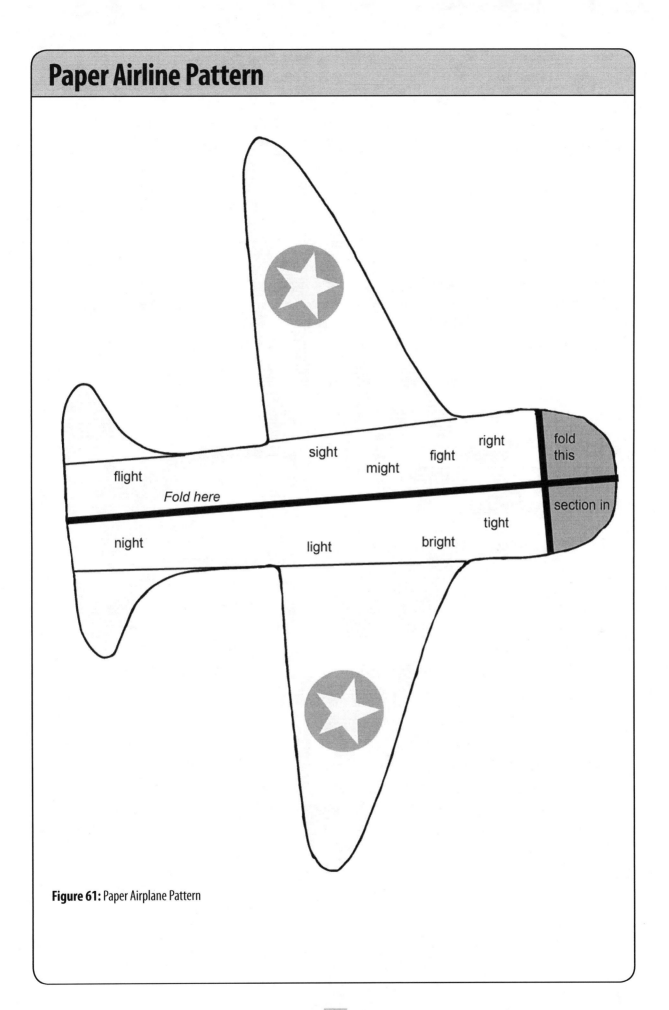

Figure 61: Paper Airplane Pattern

Unit 35: The –*et* Rime

PRESENTING THE VERSE

Use a chart, the board, or word cards to introduce the –*et* rime words, which include *bet, get, let, met, net, pet, set, wet,* and *vet.* On a chart, or on the board, write the following phrases: Met Bet, get her pet, met her pet, pet at vet, poor pet. Write each on a separate line. Point at them as they occur in the verse. Encourage the group to read them.

Bet's Pet: A Cumulative Verse

Leader: Have you ever met Bet? *Boys:* Have you ever met Bet? *Girls:* Have you ever met Bet?
Leader: What did you do? (points to chart) *All:* Met Bet.

Leader: Bet went to get her pet. *Boys:* Bet went to get her pet. *Girls:* Bet went to get her pet.
Leader: What did you do? All: Met Bet. *Leader:* Where did she go? *All:* To get her pet.

Leader: Bet's pet was at the vet. *Boys:* Bet's pet was at the vet. *Girls:* Bet's pet was at the vet.
Leader: What did you do? *All:* Met Bet. *Leader:* Where did she go? *All:* To get her pet.
Leader: Where was her pet? *All:* At the vet.

Leader: Bet's pet was very wet. *Boys:* Bet's pet was very wet. *Girls:* Bet's pet was very wet.
Leader: What did you do? *All:* Met Bet. *Leader:* Where did she go? *All:* To get her pet.
Leader: Where was her pet? *All:* At the vet. *Leader:* Why was it there? *All:* It was wet.

I Have a Pet: Activity

Materials
■ prints of various pets, including a cat, to study

Directions
1. Encourage children to share stories about pets.
2. Show them the pet prints.
3. Pointing to a cat picture, give an example of a riddle clue, "I have four legs and some people say I have nine lives, what am I?"
4. Invite volunteers to offer their clues to the group.
5. Participants may guess the identity of the mystery pet.
6. Give students time to draw a picture of a pet they have or would like to have and share their picture with the group.
7. Tell students to write about a pet. Encourage them to use at least three words from the chart.

SUGGESTED BOOKS TO COMPLETE THE PROGRAM

The Perfect Pet by Margie Palatini

Pet Show! by Ezra Jack Keats

The Best Pet of All by David LaRochelle

What Pet to Get? by Emma Dodd

APPENDICES

Appendix One: Skills Chart Based on Reading Standards

Skills

Appendix Two: Table of Common Rimes

all, ball, call, fall, hall, mall, tall, wall; **harder options:** small, stall

Dan, fan, man, Nan, pan, ran, tan; **harder option:** plan

cap, gap, lap, map, nap, rap, sap, tap, zap; **harder options:** trap, flap, snap, slap

bat, brat, cat, fat, hat, mat, Nat, pat, rat, sat, tat; **harder options:** brat, scat, flat, slat, splat

ash, bash, cash, dash, hash, mash, rash, sash; **harder options:** flash, stash, crash, trash

back, hack, lack, pack, rack, sack, tack, Zack; **harder options:** clack, crack, shack, slack, stack, smack, track

caw, law, paw, raw, saw; **harder options:** draw, flaw, straw, claw

bell, dell, fell, Nell, sell, tell, well; **harder options:** spell, smell, swell

best, nest, pest, rest, test, west, zest, fest; **harder option:** guest, quest

lick, pick, sick, tick, wick; **harder options:** flick, stick, brick, trick, slick

Bill, dill, Jill, fill, hill, pill, sill, will, mill, till; **harder options:** quill, still, spill, thrill, drill, frill king, ding, ping, ring, sing, wing; **harder options:** bring, cling, fling, string, sting, spring, swing

dip, hip, lip, sip, tip, zip; **harder options:** clip, slip, strip, chip, drip, flip, grip, snip, ship, whip, trip

bin, fin, pin, tin, win; **harder options:** chin, thin, twin, spin

link, mink, pink, rink, sink, wink; **harder options:** blink, drink, shrink, stink, think

bunk, chunk, clunk, dunk, sunk, hunk, junk; **harder options:** shrunk, slunk, flunk, trunk

dock, lock, rock, sock, tock; **harder options:** flock, knock, block, smock, shock, stock, clock

dot, got, cot, hot, lot, not, pot, rot, tot; **harder options:** trot, shot, spot, slot

bog, dog, fog, hog, log; **harder options:** frog, smog

bop, hop, mop, pop, top, crop; **harder options:** drop, flop, clop, shop, stop

bug, dug, hug, jug, lug, mug, rug, tug, pug; **harder options:** snug, chug, shrug, smug, plug

buck, duck, luck, tuck; **harder options:** cluck, Chuck, truck, stuck, struck, muck

bump, dump, hump, lump, pump, jump; **harder options:** clump, slump, stump, plump

gain, main, pain, rain, stain, train; **harder options:** drain, grain, plain, strain, Spain

bake, cake, fake, lake, make, rake, take, wake, sake; **harder options:** flake, snake, stake, mistake

bail, fail, jail, hail, mail, nail, pail, rail, sail, tail; **harder options:** frail, trail, snail

came, dame, fame, game, lame, name, same, tame; **harder options:** blame, flame, frame

date, fate, gate, hate, late, rate, mate; **harder options:** grate, slate, state, plate

bay, gay, day, hay, lay, may, pay, ray, say, way; **harder options:** bray, tray, gray, stay, play, pray, clay, stray

eat, beat, heat, meat, neat, seat; **harder options:** bleat, treat, wheat

dice, mice, nice, rice; **harder options:** price, slice, twice

hide, ride, side, tide, wide; **harder options:** bride, glide, slide, pride

fight, light, might, night, right, tight, sight; **harder options:** bright, delight, fright, flight, slight

bore, core, lore, more, tore, wore, sore; **harder options:** ignore, snore, store, swore, adore, explore

Appendix Three: Bibliography of Rhyming Picture Books and Easy Readers

Although these classic books do not feature specific rimes or word families, their rhythms, predictable patterns, and rhymes aid decoding or encourage enthusiastic group participation. Add one or two to a story hour program or place a few on a browsing table.

Adams, Pam. *Oh Soldier, Soldier, Won't You Marry Me?* New York: Child's Play International, 1990.

Adlerman, Daniel. *Africa Calling, Night Time Falling.* Watertown, MA: Charlesbridge Publishing, 2001.

Ahlberg, Allan, and Janet Ahlberg. *Each Peach Pear Plum.* Ringwood, Victoria, Australia: Puffin Books, 1999.

Ahlberg, Allan. *The Jolly Christmas Postman.* Milwaukee: LB Kids, 2001.

Apple, Margot, and Abby Levine. *You Push, I Ride.* New York City: Puffin, 1990.

Appendices (continued)

Archambault, John, and Bill Martin Jr. *Chicka Chicka Boom Boom*. New York: Little Simon, 2006.

Archambault, John, and Bill Martin. *Barn Dance!* New York: New York: Henry Holt Books for Young Readers, 1988.

Archambault, John, and Bill Martin. *Here Are My Hands*. New York: Henry Holt Books for Young Readers, 2007.

Archbold, Tim, and Claire O'Brien. *Barn Party*. New York: Kingfisher, 2005.

Arnold, Tedd. *Five Ugly Monsters*. New York: Scholastic Inc., 1998.

Aylesworth, Jim. *Old Black Fly*. New York: Henry Holt Books for Young Readers, 1995.

Base, Graeme. *Eleventh Hour*. New York: Harry N. Abrams, 1993.

Becker, John E. *Seven Little Rabbits*. New York: Walker Books for Young Readers, 2007.

Bemelmans, Ludwig. *Madeline*. Reissue of 1939 edition. New York: Viking Press, 1967.

Berenstain, Jan, and Stan Berenstain. *The Berenstain Bears and the Ghost of the Forest*. New York: Random House Books for Young Readers, 1988.

Blathwayt, Benedict. *Dinosaur Chase!* Chicago: Red Fox, 2007.

Bogart, Jo Ellen. *Gifts*. New York: Scholastic Trade, 1996.

Bouchard, David. *If You're Not from the Prairie*. Vancouver: Raincoast Books, 2002.

Boynton, Sandra. *Pajama Time!* Chicago: Workman Publishing Company, 2000.

Brooke, L. Leslie. *Johnny Crow's Garden*. London: Warne, 1986.

Brown, Margaret Wise. *Goodnight Moon*. 60th Anniversary Edition. New York: HarperCollins, 2005.

Bunting, Eve. *Scary, Scary Halloween*. New York: Clarion Books, 1988.

Bunting, Eve. *The Mother's Day Mice*. New York: Clarion Books, 1988.

Capucilli, Alyssa Satin. *Inside a Barn in the Country: A Rebus Read-Along Story*. New York: Scholastic, 1995.

Carlstrom, Nancy White. *Better Not Get Wet, Jesse Bear*. New York: Aladdin, 1997.

Carlstrom, Nancy White. *What a Scare, Jesse Bear*. New York: Aladdin, 2002.

Chandra, Deborah. *Miss Mabel's Table*. New York: Harcourt, 1994.

Chase, Edith Newlin. *The New Baby Calf*. New York: Scholastic Paperbacks, 1992.

Cochrane, Orin, and Terry Gallagher. *Cinderella Chant*. Sai Kung Hong Kong: Whole Language Consultants Ltd., 1988.

Cohen, Charles D., and Dr. Seuss. *How the Grinch Stole Christmas—Anniversary Edition: A 50th Anniversary Retrospective*. New York: Random House Books for Young Readers, 2007.

Cullen, Catherine Ann. *Thirsty Baby*. Boston: Little, Brown, 2003.

Dalton, Anne. *This Is the Way*. New York: Scholastic Trade, 1992.

David, Kirk. *Miss Spider's Sunny Patch Kids*. New York: Scholastic, 2004.

De Paola, Tomie. *Tomie De Paola's Mother Goose Favorites*. New York: Tandem Library, 2000.

Degen, Bruce. *Jamberry*. New York: HarperCollins, 1983.

Deming, A. G. *Who Is Tapping at My Window?* New York: Puffin, 1994.

Diterlizzi, Tony, and Mary Howitt. *The Spider and the Fly*. New York: Simon & Schuster Children's Publishing, 2002.

Dodds, Dayle Ann. *Wheel Away!* New York: HarperCollins Children's Books, 1991.

Dragonwagon, Crescent. *Alligator Arrived with Apples: A Potluck Alphabet Feast*. New York: Aladdin, 1992.

Dunbar, Joyce. *Four Fierce Kittens*. New York: Orchard Books, 1992.

Dunbar, Joyce. *Ten Little Mice*. London: Voyager Books, 1995.

Eastman, P.D. *The Best Nest*. New York: Random House Books for Young Readers, 1968.

Edwards, Pamela Duncan. *Four Famished Foxes and Fosdyke*. New York: HarperTrophy, 1997.

Ehlert, Lois. *Eating the Alphabet: Fruits & Vegetables from A to Z*. London: Voyager Books, 1993.

Emberley, Barbara. *One Wide, River to Cross*. New York: Little Brown & Co, 1992.

Evans, Dilys. *Monster Soup: And Other Spooky Poems*. New York: Cartwheel Books (Scholastics), 1995.

Fleming, Denise. *In the Small, Small Pond*. New York: Henry Holt Books for Young Readers, 2007.

Fleming, Denise. *In the Tall, Tall Grass*. New York: Henry Holt Books for Young Readers, 1993.

Fleming, Denise. *Lunch*. New York: Henry Holt Books for Young Readers, 1996.

Fleming, Denise. *Time to Sleep*. New York: Henry Holt Books for Young Readers, 1997.

Florian, Douglas. *Bing Bang Boing*. New York: Harcourt Children's Books, 1994.

Fortunata. *Catch a Little Fox*. New York: Scholastic Book Services, 1968.

Fox, Mem. *Time for Bed*. Singapore: Gulliver Books, 1993.

Fox, Mem. *Whoever You Are*. London: Voyager Books, 2006.

Frances and Father Jean De Brebeuf Tyrell. *The Huron Carol*. New York: Dutton, 1990.

Freeman, Don. *Mop Top*. Pueblo: Live Oak Media, 1982.

Gag, Wanda. *The ABC Bunny*. Minneapolis: University of Minnesota Press, 2004.

Galdone, Paul. *Henny Penny*. New York: Clarion Books, 1984.

Garland, Michael. *The Mouse before Christmas*. New York: Scholastic, Inc., 2004.

Geisel, Theodore, and Dr. Seuss. *Fox in Socks*. New York: Random House, Inc., 1965.

Gelman, Rita Golden. *Hello, Cat, You Need a Hat*. New York: Cartwheel Books (Scholastics), 1999.

Gerrard, Roy. *Rosie and the Rustlers*. New York: Farrar, Straus and Giroux Books for Young Readers, 1991.

Gilman, Phoebe. *Jillian Jiggs to the Rescue*. New York: Scholastic Trade, 1994.

Giogas, Valarie. *In My Backyard*. Mt. Pleasant, SC: Sylvan Dell Publishing, 2007.

Golick, Margie. *Wacky Word Games*. Toronto: Pembroke Pub Ltd, 2001.

Goodman, Yetta Trachtman. *The Little Overcoat: Traditional Folksong*. Greenvale, NY: Mondo Publishing, 1998.

Gordon, Jeffie Ross. *Six Sleepy Sheep*. New York: Puffin, 1993.

Guarino, Deborah. *Is Your Mama a Llama?* New York: Scholastic Audio, 1990.

Gunson, Christopher. *Over on the Farm*. Buffalo: Red Fox Books (Rand), 2003.

Harrison, David L. *When Cows Come Home*. Honesdale, PA: Boyds Mills Press, 2001.

Hawkins, Colin, and Jacqui Hawkins. *Tog the Dog Literacy Hour Pack*. London: Dorling Kindersley Publishers Ltd., 2001.

Hayes, Sarah. *This Is the Bear and the Picnic Lunch*. New York: Walker Books Ltd., 2003.

Hennessy, B.G. *Jake Baked the Cake*. New York: Puffin, 1992.

Hoberman, Mary Ann. *A House Is a House for Me*. New York: Puffin, 2007.

Hoffman, Hilde. *Green Grass Grows All Around*. New York: Macmillan Publishing Company, 1968.

Hopkins, Lee Bennett. *Blast Off! Poems about Space*. New York: HarperCollins Children's Books, 1995.

Hort, Lenny. *The Seals on the Bus*. New York: Owlet Paperbacks, 2003.

Jorgensen, Gail. *Crocodile Beat*. New York: Aladdin, 1994.

Keats, Ezra Jack. *Over in the Meadow*. New York: Puffin, 1999.

Kennedy, Jimmy. *Teddy Bears' Picnic*. New York: Aladdin, 2000.

King, Bob. *Sitting on the Farm*. Fort Worth: Harcourt Brace College Publishers, 1995.

Kirk, Daniel. *Trash Trucks*. USA: Troll, 1997.

Kirk, David. *Miss Spider's Tea Party*. New York: Scholastic Inc., 2007.

Krauss, Ruth. *I Can Fly*. Barnstaple, U.K.: Golden Books, 2003.

Kuskin, Karla. *Roar and More*. Honesdale, PA: Boyds Mills Press, 2004.

Lesieg, Theo. *Maybe You Should Fly a Jet! Maybe You Should Be a Vet!* Troy: Picture Lions, 2001.

Leuck, Laura. *Sun Is Falling, Night Is Calling*. New York: Simon & Schuster Children's Publishing, 1994.

Lewison, Wendy Cheyette. *Buzz Said the Bee*. New York: Cartwheel, 1992.

Lindbergh, Reeve. *The Day the Goose Got Loose*. New York: Puffin, 1995.

Lindbergh, Reeve. *There's a Cow in the Road!* New York: Dial, 1993.

Lobel, Arnold. *On Market Street*. 25th Anniversary Edition. New York: HarperTrophy, 1989.

Mandel, Peter. *Red Cat White Cat*. New York: Henry Holt & Co, 1994.

Marshall, James. *Old Mother Hubbard and Her Wonderful Dog*. New York: Farrar, Straus and Giroux Books for Young Readers, 1993.

Martin Jr., Bill. *Old Devil Wind*. London: Voyager Books, 1996.

Martin, Bill. *Polar Bear, Polar Bear, What Do You Hear?* New York: Henry Holt and Co. Books for Young Readers, 1992.

Martin, Bill. *The Braggin' Dragon*. Milwaukee: Trumpet Club, 1993.

Marzollo, Jean. *I'm Tyrannosaurus! A Book of Dinosaur Rhymes*. New York: Scholastic Inc., 1999.

Marzollo, Jean. *Sun Song*. New York: HarperTrophy, 1997.

Marzollo, Jean. *Ten Cats Have Hats*. New York: Cartwheel Books, 1994.

Mcphail, David. *Pigs Aplenty, Pigs Galore!* New York: Puffin, 1996.

McPherson, Jan. *Jennifer Pockets*. New York: Wright Group/McGraw-Hill, 1992.

Milios, Rita. *Bears, Bears, Everywhere*. New York: Children's Press, 2003.

Miranda, Anne. *To Market, To Market*. London: Voyager Books, 2001.

Molnar, Gwen. *I Said to Sam*. New York: Scholastic, 1987.

Morrison, Bill. *Squeeze a Sneeze*. Boston: Houghton Mifflin, 1987.

Muller, Robin. *Hickory, Dickory, Dock*. Markham, Ontario: Scholastic Canada, 2005.

Muntz, Percival. *Double Trouble*. New York: Cartwheel, 2005.

Neitzel, Shirley. *We're Making Breakfast for Mother*. New York: Greenwillow, 1997.

Novelli, Joan. *Teaching with the Rib-Tickling Poetry of Douglas Florian*. New York: Teaching Resources, 2003.

Ochs, Carol Partridge. *Moose on the Loose*. Minneapolis: Carolrhoda Books, 1991.

Pallotta, Jerry, and Pam Munoz Ryan. *The Crayon Counting Book*. Watertown, MA: Charlesbridge Publishing, 1996.

Paraskevas, Betty. *Monster Beach*. New York: Harcourt, 1995.

Parkes, Brenda. *The Gingerbread Man*. San Francisco: Mimosa Publications, 2001.

Patron, Susan. *Dark Cloud Strong Breeze*. New York: Orchard Books, 1994.

Patz, Nancy. *Moses Supposes His Toeses Are Roses: And 7 Other Silly Old Rhymes*. London: Voyager Books, 1989.

Peet, Bill. *Kermit the Hermit*. Boston: Houghton Mifflin, 1980.

Pelham, David. *Sam's Pizza*. New York: Dutton Juvenile, 1996.

Pelham, David. *Sam's Sandwich*. New York: Dutton Juvenile, 1991.

Pinezes, Elinor. *One Hundred Hungry Ants*. New York: Scholastic Inc., 1997.

Pomerantz, Charlotte. *Flap Your Wings and Try*. New York: Greenwillow, 1989.

Pomerantz, Charlotte. *If I Had a Paka*. New York: HarperTrophy, 1993.

Prelutsky, Jack. *Behold the Bold Umbrellaphant: And Other Poems*. New York: Greenwillow, 2006.

Prelutsky, Jack. *For Laughing Out Loud: Poems to Tickle Your Funnybone*. New York: Knopf Books for Young Readers, 1991.

Prelutsky, Jack. *It's Raining Pigs & Noodles*. New York: HarperTrophy, 2005.

Punnett, Dick. *Our Brat Cat: Double Rhyme Books*. Chanhassen, MN: Child's World, 1985.

Raeside, Adrian. *Dennis and the Fantastic Forest*. Toronto: Doubleday Canada, Limited, 1997.

Raffi. *Baby Beluga*. New York: Crown Books for Young Readers, 1992.

Raffi. *Down by the Bay*. New York: Crown Books for Young Readers, 1988.

Raffi. *Shake My Sillies Out*. New York: Crown Books for Young Readers, 1988.

Raffi. *Spider on the Floor*. New York: Crown Books for Young Readers, 1996.

Raffi. *Tingalayo*. New York: Dragonfly Books, 1993.

Raffi. *The Wheels on the Bus*. New York: Crown Books for Young Readers, 1990.

Regniers, Beatrice Schenk De. *Sing a Song of Popcorn*. New York: Hodder & Stoughton Children's Division, 1988.

Reid, Barbara. *The Party*. New York: Scholastic, 1999.

Robinson, Martha. *The Zoo at Night*. Chicago: Margaret K. McElderry, 1995.

Root, Phyllis. *One Duck Stuck*. Cambridge: Candlewick, 2003.

Schade, Susan. *I Love You, Good Night*. New York: Little Simon, 1990.

Schnetzler, Pattie. *Ten Little Dinosaurs*. Denver: Accord Publishing, 2000.

Sendak, Maurice. *Chicken Soup with Rice*. New York: Scholastic Book Services, 1968.

Seuss, Dr. *Dr. Seuss's Sleep Book*. New York: Random House Books for Young Readers, 1962.

Seuss, Dr. *Great Day for Up!* New York: Random House Books for Young Readers, 1974.

Seuss, Dr. *Green Eggs and Ham*. New York: Random House Books for Young Readers, 1987.

Seuss, Dr. *Hop on Pop*. Book and CD. New York: Random House Books for Young Readers, 2005.

Seuss, Dr. *Horton Hears a Who!* New York: Random House Books for Young Readers, 1954.

Seuss, Dr. *I Can Read with My Eyes Shut!* New York: Random House Books for Young Readers, 1978.

Seuss, Dr. *If I Ran the Zoo*. New York: Random House Books for Young Readers, 1950.

Seuss, Dr. *One Fish, Two Fish, Red Fish, Blue Fish*. Book and CD. New York: Random House Books for Young Readers, 2005.

Seuss, Dr. *The Cat in the Hat*. Book and Audiocassette. New York: Random House Books for Young Readers, 1987.

Seuss, Dr. *The Foot Book: Dr. Seuss's Wacky Book of Opposites*. New York: Random House Books for Young Readers, 1996.

Seuss, Dr. *There's a Wocket in My Pocket!* New York: Random House Books for Young Readers, 1974.

Shapiro, Arnold. *Mice Squeak, We Speak*. New York: Putnam Juvenile, 1997.

Shaw, Nancy E. *Sheep Take a Hike*. Boston: Houghton Mifflin, 1996.

Shaw, Nancy E. *Sheep in a Jeep*. Book and CD. Boston: Houghton Mifflin, 2006.

Shaw, Nancy E. *Sheep in a Shop*. Boston: Houghton Mifflin, 1994.

Siebert, Diane. *Train Song*. New York: HarperTrophy, 1993.

Silverstein, Shel. *A Light in the Attic*. 20th Anniversary Edition Book and CD. New York: HarperCollins, 2001.

Silverstein, Shel. *Falling Up*. New York: HarperCollins, 1996.

Silverstein, Shel. *Where the Sidewalk Ends*. 25th Anniversary Edition Book and CD. New York: HarperCollins, 2000.

Sloat, Teri. *Thing That Bothered Farmer Brown*. New York: Scholastic Inc., 2001.

Smith, Barry. *The Carousel at Scarborough Fair*. London: Trafalgar Square, 1996.

Spier, Peter. *The Fox Went Out on a Chilly Night*. New York: Dragonfly Books, 1994.

Staines, Bill. *All God's Critters Got a Place in the Choir*. New York: Puffin, 1993.

Stickland, Paul. *One Bear, One Dog*. Andover, MA: Ragged Bears, 2005.

Seuss, Dr. Dr. Seuss Beginner Books: *The Cat in the Hat; Go, Dog. Go!; Dr. Seuss's ABC; Oh the Thinks You Can Think; Fox in Socks*. New York: Random House, 1980.

Szekeres, Cyndy. *The Mouse That Jack Built*. New York: Scholastic, 1997.

Taback, Simms. *There Was an Old Lady Who Swallowed a Fly*. New York: Scholastic Inc., 1999.

Tafuri, Nancy. *Early Morning in the Barn*. New York: Mulberry Books, 1992.

Thomas, Jan. *What Will Fat Cat Sit On?* New York: Harcourt Children's Books, 2007.

Trapani, Iza. *Twinkle, Twinkle, Little Star*. Watertown, MA: Charlesbridge Publishing, 1997.

Turner, Gwenda. *Over on the Farm*. New York: Viking Juvenile, 1994.

Unwin, Nora Spicer. *Two Too Many*. New York: D. McKay Co, 1962.

Vaughan, Marcia K. *Wombat Stew*. New York: Scholastic Inc., 1998.

Weiss, Nicki. *Sun Sand Sea Sail*. New Jersey: Random House Value Publishing, 1991.

Appendices (continued)

Wellington, Monica. *Night House Bright House*. New York: Dutton Juvenile, 1997.

Wells, Rosemary. *Bingo!* New York: Scholastic Press, 1999.

West, Colin. *I Bought My Love a Tabby Cat*. New Jersey: Random House Value Publishing, 1990.

Williams, Rozanne Lanczak. *The Giraffe Made Her Laugh*. Huntington Beach: Creative Teaching Press, 1994.

Williams, Rozanne Lanczak. *There's a Monster in the Tree*. Huntington Beach: Creative Teaching Press, 1995.

Wood, Audrey. *Silly Sally*. New York: Scholastic Inc., 1995.

Wood, Audrey. *The Napping House*. Book and CD. New York: Harcourt Children's Books, 2004.

Wright, Joan Richards. *Bugs*. New York: HarperTrophy, 1988.

Young, James. *Cows Are in the Corn*. New York: Scholastic Inc., 1995.

Zemach, Harve. *The Judge: An Untrue Tale*. New York: Farrar, Straus and Giroux Books for Young Readers, 1969.

Zemach, Margot. *Hush, Little Baby*. New York: EP Dutton, 1976.

Appendix Four: Bibliography of Professional Books about Rimes and Reading

Need more theoretical information, assessment tools, or additional verses? Try these outstanding references.

Fox, Barbara J. *Phonics for the Teacher of Reading (9th Edition)*. Alexandria, VA: Prentice Hall, 2005. This self-guided journey through the world of phonics is perfect for the busy professional looking for an introduction to the subject, or a quick review.

Fry, Ed, Dr. and Daphne Ransom. *Dr. Fry's Informal Reading Assessments*. Westminster, CA: Teacher Created Resources, 2001. This classic belongs in every collection. It helps teachers and parents hone in on strengths and weaknesses quickly and efficiently.

Lane, Holly B., and Paige C. Pullen. *Phonological Awareness Assessment and Instruction: A Sound Beginning*. Boston, MA: Allyn & Bacon, 2003. Based on recent research, this resource offers theoretical background, as well as suggestions for effective testing and skills remediation.

Rasinski, Timothy V., and Belinda S. Zimmerman. *Phonics Poetry: Teaching Word Families*. Boston, MA: Allyn & Bacon, 2000. This useful book includes about 100 verses, along with suggestions for teaching rimes.

Sweeney, Alyse. *Teaching the Essentials of Reading with Picture Books: 15 Lessons That Use Favorite Picture Books to Teach Phonemic Awareness, Phonics, Fluency, Comprehension, and Vocabulary*. Chicago: Scholastic Professional Books, 2004. These excellent lessons can be used as-is, or as jumping-off points for your own ideas.

Appendix Five: Table of Useful Web Sites

A longitudinal study of the effects of word frequency and rime-neighborhood size on beginning readers' rime reading accuracy in words and non-words.

Journal of Literacy Research. Mar 2002 by Calhoon, J Anne, Leslie, Lauren
        <findarticles.com/p/articles/mi_qa3785/is_200203/ai_n9066153>

Annenberg Media, Learner.org: Teaching Reading K-2
        <www.learner.org/channel/libraries/readingk2/front/otherterms.html>

Click, Clack, Moo: Reading Word Family Words:
        <www.readwritethink.org/lessons/lesson_view.asp?id=847>

Phonemic analysis and reading development: some current issues:
        <www.blackwell-synergy.com/doi/abs/10.1111/j.1467-9817.2005.00251.x>

Put Reading First: The Research Building Blocks for Teaching Children to Read:
        <www.nifl.gov/partnershipforreading/publications/reading_first1.html>

Rhyming With Seuss: Emergent Literacy
        <www.auburn.edu/academic/education/reading_genie/connect/mcwilliamsel.html>

Rimes and Rhymes:
        <www.teach.virginia.edu/go/wil/rimes_and_rhymes.htm>

Silly Kindergarten By: Amanda Post
        <atozteacherstuff.com/pages/415.shtml>

Small versus large unit theories of reading acquisition:
        <www3.interscience.wiley.com/cgibin/abstract/15402/abstract?cretry=1&sretry=0>

Teaching Rimes with Shared Reading by Sharon Ruth Gill, International Reading Association site:
        <www.reading.org/publications/journals/rt/v60/i2/abstracts/RT-60-2-Gill.html>

Teaching Short Vowel Discrimination Using Dr. Seuss Rhymes:
        <www.readwritethink.org/lessons/lesson_view.asp?id=113>

The effects of Rhyme-Rime Connection training on second-grade reading performance by Melinda Lea
        Smith, Oklahoma State University:
        <e-archive.library.okstate.edu/dissertations/AAI3057310/>

You've Got a Wocket Where?
        <www.teachers.net/lessons/posts/1062.html.

Index